God-Like Engineering-II:

Life and Death

RK Samson

Title: God-Like Engineering-II: Life and Death

Author: RK Samson

Published by Metaphysics Christ Foundation

Bangalore, India

ISBN: 978-81-995115-9-0

Edition: First Edition

Dedication

This book is humbly dedicated to the selfless workers of the Gospel, who suffered quietly, were persecuted deeply, and died for the sake of their higher calling.

Contents

PREFACE

We learned in the book, "God-like Engineering-I" that the seals of God are in man as signs of God. A summary of this is provided below.

1) Great philosophers such as Plato and Thiruvalluvar stated that there exists something real in every unreal thing. This Real thing is nothing more than God-like things as divinity.
2) As per great scientists, God's nature is revealed through His mind that He used to create every creation.
3) According to Islam, God created man in order to enable him to know God. So we've seen that man has God-like things as divinity.
4) According to Hinduism, every man has divine qualities. This is known as divinity.
5) Judaism says that man is created as per the likeness and image of God. So we've seen that man has God-like things as divinity.

6) Christianity says that man is created as per the likeness and image of God. So we've seen that man has God-like things as divinity.

Together, these voices resound like a symphony, proclaiming that the entire cosmos reflects the likeness of God, and every human being carries His seal—a divine model that transcends time, culture, and creed.

Yet, the mystery deepens: just as God is triune—Father, Son, and Holy Spirit—so too is humanity triune in essence. Within every creation lies a testimony, a silent yet powerful sermon proclaiming, "Christ is the Creator God." Across the globe, this inherent truth stirs within every heart, whether consciously recognized or not.

This revelation fills us with awe and thrilling expectation. If every breath we take, every thought we ponder, and every longing in our soul points to the One True God, then we are not merely wanderers in a cosmic accident—we are purposeful creations, destined to know, worship, and glorify the Living God. Such knowledge ignites a fire of bliss and hope, lifting us beyond the mundane into the divine.

And yet, there is a sobering truth: when humanity turns its worship to the finite, the mortal, or the created—ignoring the Creator—it courts the very wrath of God. *God-like Engineering-I* warned us of this peril, urging us to fix our eyes on the eternal and to honor the One who alone is worthy of worship.

As we now stand on the threshold of *God-like Engineering-II*, let our hearts soar with expectation. What greater joy can there be than to explore deeper into the mystery of God's design in us? What greater thrill than to discover how the Creator's fingerprints shape not only our being but the entire universe? Prepare to be inspired, to be moved, to encounter the Triune God whose love and power know no bounds.

Let this journey lead us into the fullness of our divine calling, as we stand in awe of God who created us in His image, sealed us with His essence, and invites us into eternal communion with Him. This is more than knowledge—it is an invitation to transformation, an encounter with the living God who is the source of all truth, beauty, and bliss. The adventure awaits as you read and understand this book!

WHY SUFFERINGS?

God took the utmost care while creating man. Scripture teaches that man was fearfully and wonderfully made (Psalm 139: 14)

Psalms 139:14 I will praise thee; for I am fearfully and wonderfully made: marvellous are thy works; and that my soul knoweth right well

Why does man's life, though created by God, be illusory? Why is there so much trouble in man's life? These are the most important questions could be raised by many. Why did the man who was designed after God Himself, troubled his life as we see below?

1) Why is man running straight to destruction?

2) Why does man suffer?

3) Why is man's condition worse if he has a God?

4) Why does the state of misery that we are experiencing now last?

5) Why are there ups and downs within society?

6) Why there are poor and rich?

7) Why are there evil people?

8) Why does Karma (sin) chase man?

9) Why does death occur?

10) Why does the illusion persist?

11) Why do tears, fear, anxiety and stress persist?

12) Why does ignorance persist?

13) Why does man's nudity last?

14) Why do murder, robbery, adultery, theft, lying, hypocrisy, and disobedience persist?

15) Why do hard efforts to go near God persist?

16) Why is life in darkness without knowing the future?

17) Why do so many mysteries remain in man's life?

There is only one answer to all these questions. God created human beings with his own likeness and guaranteed beautiful and peaceful life. But man destroyed some of his God-like seals (God-like signs) in him. The destruction of God-like seals meant that the man lost his guarantee of his life and eternal life. This is why man's life has become troubled. Shovel all the problems and questions of the world into the seal of God (Likeness of God), this is the only place to find solutions to all the problems and questions.

The Lord did not create man and the fellow creatures wrong. All the divine seals were fine in man on the day the man was created. The man was neat and tidy. But the terrible consequences were reported only when man broke the seal of God in him. So, in the world that exists now, man lives as living in hell.

Now, we are going to see how the first man had likeness and image of God as seals, how the first man damaged important seals, what are the deadly consequences reported after damaging the God's seals, how the seals are restored and how all the sufferings of mankind come to an end. All these are detailed in this book.

In this book, we are going to see the following:

1) What are the most important seals of the God?

2) How horroful terrors caused by the cracking of seals?

3) How deaths caused by the cracking of the seal?

4) What are the hurdles against retrieval of divine seals?

5) The migration of Conscience

6) Court of conscience

7) The rule of conscience

8) The hurdle called Dead-Karma

9) Major efforts to eliminate hurdles

10) Failures of major efforts

11) The destroyer of the obstacles that appeared with response of nature

12) The way the obstacles are removed

13) The way to get important God-like seals

14) Change in the plight of human beings

15) Destruction of illusion etc.,

God-like Engineering-II is far more significant as much as God-like Engineering-I.

❖

THE ADVENTURES OF GOD'S SEAL

Look deep into nature, and then you will understand everything better. -Albert Einstein

Nature is a volume of which God is the author. -William Harvey

Those who dwell among the beauties and mysteries of the earth are never alone or weary of life.- Rachel Carson

Amazing nature does not describe itself; rather, it reveals its Creator. God has placed His marks—His seals—in both nature and humanity. These signs reveal who God is and carry great significance throughout the world. They clearly display aspects of God: the details of His nature, His methods of action, the design of His creation, and even the image of God Himself.

Nature holds many mysteries. Throughout history, ancient philosophers, modern scientists, and major religions have sought to understand them. People from different faiths often claim, "Our teacher gave us the perfect revelation," or, "Your scriptures are wrong; only ours contain the absolute truth," or, "Only our prophet received the final revelation."

However, no matter how many books exist, the Book of Nature reveals truths more accurate than any religious text. The Book of Nature cannot be proven wrong—it declares who God is and what He is like.

In the world, every company that makes a product carefully stamps its seal of ownership on that product. This seal guarantees quality and serves as the company's identity. In the same way, God has placed His seals throughout creation. Let's continue to explore the importance of these seals—both those made by humans and those of God.

The Significance Of A Seal Of Ownership

- A seal represents legality; it shows that something is legally recognized.
- The seal offers a guarantee of quality.
- It signifies professionalism.
- It serves as an official mark.
- It is essential for publishing official documents and releasing products.
- A seal reflects brand identity.
- It informs the world about the manufacturer's identity.

- A sealed product belongs to the owner of the seal, proving that only they have rightful ownership.
- If someone falsely claims ownership, the seal helps prove the true owner and supports legal action.

Most importantly, seals carry emotional value; the care and pride of the maker are deeply connected to it.

No reputable company exists without a trademark. Seals are essential. Similarly, the Creator Lord has sealed His creatures with His own signs. Every person carries the Creator's trademark.

What Should the Design of the Divine Seals Be?

A trademark's design reflects the maker's tastes, actions, governance, attitude, problem-solving ability, benefits, and future plans. Likewise, the divine seal should be self-contained, unique, and full of emotion. If a seal includes all these qualities, it is the perfect seal. Nothing is missing in the Creator God's seal, which is present both in nature and in humanity. The Creator designed His seal and impressed it on every creature.

These seals help us recognize the Creator as the true owner of every living thing. A seal serves many purposes: recognition, license, authority, identity, and insignia.

Governments require company logos and names to be displayed on signs in front of their buildings. Millions of factories, educational and medical institutions, government agencies, charities, and places of worship from all religions inscribe their names and logos on signboards. These signs reveal the identity of the company or institution and its owner. While people who have not created anything are still careful about their organizations, we will see how God, who created everything, has been even more deliberate in setting His marks in His creations.

Take, for example, the Amazon company logo. The yellow arrow starts from the letter 'a' and ends at 'z,' showing that the company sells everything from A to Z. This arrow also looks like a smile, symbolizing the happiness of customers buying from Amazon. This logo carefully shows the company's purpose, promise, identity, and license.

Companies treat their logos as importantly as their products. Likewise, the Creator Lord has inscribed His Divine Seal on all His creations. When a company designs and manufactures a product, its name and logo are engraved or printed on it. Companies value their products, and they equally value their hallmarks. Similarly, God, who designed His creatures, has carefully inscribed His seal on everything He has made.

During weddings, the bride and groom wear rings. When a husband wears the wife's ring, the world knows he belongs to her. When a wife wears her husband's ring, the world knows she belongs to him. Marriage symbols exist in many cultures as signs of belonging.

Some people tattoo the names or images of their loved ones on their bodies to show their connection. Land deeds have owners' names and official seals to prove ownership. Land without a name or seal belongs to no one. Anonymous, unsigned, or unstamped documents are invalid.

Currency carries the symbol of its nation, and that seal grants it power in trade. Atheists have come to realize that the universe must have been designed. Would the owner of such a grand universe not leave his mark in it? Indeed, He has. All religions declare this as divine truth. We will explore this in more detail. There are millions of gods worshiped around the world. But which among them truly belongs here? Whose seal marks this world? Whose identity does this world bear? Which god does this world truly follow?

Humans carefully mark their work to show ownership. Even those who do not create use marks for their organizations. God, who created everything, has also placed His divine identity in nature. This is what humans recognize as the divinity in nature.

THE ROOT OF ALL MISERIES

Never violate the sacredness of your individual self-respect.- Theodore Parker Clergy man & Social Reformer

Self-respect knows no consideration – Mahatma Gandhi

India believes in peace but not at the cost of self-respect- Narendra Modi, Prime Minister of India

God's Seals In All Creation

God has placed His seals on everything He created, and these seals hold far greater significance than any human-made commercial marks. Humans fiercely protect their self-respect, as do nations. In the same way, God's self-respect is deeply tied to the seals He has woven into humanity. This world is saturated with God's seals—there is no place untouched by them. From the tiniest subatomic particles to the vast universe, God's marks are everywhere.

We see these seals most clearly in humans. They represent God's own self-respect, which He will never remove or replace. To destroy or replace these divine seals is to attack God's very dignity. Even ordinary people who have not created anything still carry a strong sense of self-respect. How much greater then must be God's self-respect, who created and sustains all things? God's anger burns hot against mankind because people constantly destroy or tamper with the seals He placed in them. Anyone who damages or replaces God's seals will face His righteous wrath.

Why Danger Flares During Atomic Decay

What terrible consequences occur when God's seals are changed? Consider the example of the atom, the fundamental building block of all matter in the universe. Nothing exists without atoms—from water, air, earth, stones, metals, plants, animals, birds, to human bodies.

In the book God-like Engineering IV, it is shown that the likeness of the Triune God—the Father, Son, and Holy Spirit—is embedded in every creation. When an atom or its nucleus is damaged, the divine seal within it is broken. This releases gamma, alpha, and beta rays which wreak havoc on living beings and the environment. These rays act like the burning flames of God's wrath, destroying all they touch. Atomic weapons work on this principle, bringing catastrophic destruction. The atomic bombs that leveled Hiroshima and Nagasaki shattered the divine seal within atomic nuclei. Even today, the sorrow caused by this devastation remains felt in those cities.

Why Does God's Anger Flare Against Murder?

The Father, Son, and Holy Spirit form one Triune God. Humans—composed of spirit, soul, and body—bear the seal of this Triune God, regardless of their religion. This is because the Triune God created them and engraved His divine seal within them.When a person is murdered, the spirit, soul, and body are violently separated, and the seal of God in man is broken. No one has the right to violate this sacred seal. God's wrath is ignited when His seal is distorted in this way.

The Bible says in Genesis 9:6, "Whoever sheds man's blood, by man his blood shall be shed; for in the image of God He made man." Cain was cursed for killing his brother, because he broke the seal of God in him (Genesis 4:11). The scriptures teach that murderers deserve death (Leviticus 24:17).

The consequences of murder are severe. No one should ever defile the sacred seal of God in humanity without suffering divine judgment. God's self-respect is bound up in these seals.

Why Does God Stand Against Suicide?

In God's eyes, murder and suicide are the same sin. When a person takes their own life, just as when they are murdered, their spirit, soul, and body are divided, and the seal of the Triune God is broken. No one has the authority to destroy this divine seal.

God's wrath burns against those who kill or commit suicide. Like murder, suicide carries dreadful consequences. The greatest sins in this world arise from damaging or destroying the seals of the true God.

The Meaning Of The Destruction Of Man

God created humans as a reflection of Himself. Man's constitution, design, and nature all mirror the likeness of God. When any part of this design is broken or distorted—such as the separation of spirit, soul, and body—it means the seal of the Triune God in man is destroyed.

This separation and destruction are what we call death. Death is not just a physical event; it is the ruin of God's image in humanity.

***

THE COLLAPSE OF LIFE'S DESIGN

God designed every system in the human body, soul, and spirit as a seal. Each system represents a seal. If one or more of these systems is broken, then God's seal or seals are broken. When God's seal is broken, humans face devastating consequences. When a person is murdered, it separates the soul, spirit, and body, breaking the seal and disrupting the eternal order. Until today, mankind has experienced catastrophic results from this. Adam shattered two major seals, plunging all humanity into irreversible misery. In this chapter, we will learn how and when Adam broke two important seals of God.

The First Major Seal Of God

Though God the Father, who is soul-like, is invisible, He is the true God. He gives life to His body-like Jesus Christ. Every word of God originates from the Father. The Father performs good deeds, and the love of God originates from Him. Moreover, He glorifies the body-like Jesus. He also serves as the Master, Lord, and Ruler and is greater than Jesus Christ. Every gift, secret, and plan come from the Father.

Therefore, Jesus Christ placed the Father in a lofty position, obeyed Him, and accomplished the Father's will. In the same way, the human physical body must obey the soul. This is God's likeness. The human soul is invisible yet is the true person. The human body must exalt the soul, submit to it, and carry out its will. When the body obeys the soul, it reflects the image of God.

Ephesians 5:1 says, "Become followers of God, as beloved children." In Greek, "follow" is mimetus (μιμητής), meaning "to imitate." Even the philosopher Plato said, "Every creature imitates the Real One (God)." To imitate God is to act like God. Man should never change this divine seal. Every person should imitate God. This is God's eternal order, a natural and supernatural law written in every human being. No one is authorized to change it.

When Adam was created, his soul and body were in the likeness of the Father and Jesus Christ. Just as Jesus Christ honored and obeyed the Father, Adam's physical body honored and obeyed his soul. Adam's body spoke the words of his soul and did only its will. Because of this obedience, Adam's body and soul reflected the likeness of God.

Adam Damaged The First Major Seal

When Adam sinned, his fleshly body manifested itself as the real man, without concern for the soul. As a result, his soul became a servant of the physical body and fulfilled the will of the flesh. This is how Adam's soul was transformed into a worker for his physical body.

The physical body that conquered the soul dictated to the soul its desires and lusts. The soul devised a plan based on the needs and lusts of the flesh, and mobilized the physical body to work for the same purpose. Man should not be led by his body. It is not the God's likeness. Furthermore, the flesh does not have a clean attitude. The works of the flesh are sinful.

Galatians 5:19-21 Now the works of the flesh are manifest, which are these; Adultery, fornication, uncleanness, lasciviousness, Idolatry, witchcraft, hatred, variance, emulations, wrath, strife, seditions, heresies, Envying, murders, drunkenness, reveling, and such like: of the which I tell you before, as I have also told you in time past, that they which do such things shall not inherit the kingdom of God.

Today, the entire world is in misery because man modified his working likeness to be different from God's working likeness. There was no sin in the earth as long as Adam's soul, body, and spirit functioned as the Father, Son, and Holy Spirit. The world was wonderful and peaceful.

Do you understand why there is so much unrest in the world? Do you know why the world is so rotten today? This is because man did not behave in accordance with the operating mechanism of his Creator. Man lost his active resemblance to God, which means he harmed the Creator's own seal, which was interwoven in man.

The Second Major Seal Of God

The Trinity, God's soul-like Father directs His Holy Spirit. God the Father directs the Holy Spirit by directing him where to go, why to go, how much to go, and how long to go. The Holy Spirit performs the will of the soul-like Father, not the will of the physical body-like Jesus Christ. God the Father does not do what the Holy Spirit says. As the scriptures reveal, the Holy Spirit only acts in accordance with the Father. We have learned more about this in detail through God-like Engineering – I.

The souls of men must lead their spirit, just as the Holy Spirit is lead by the Father. The spirit of man should not lead its soul. Human soul should lead the spirit by telling where to go, for what reason to go, to what measure to go, and for how long to go. Human spirit should do the will of the soul, not the will of the fleshy body. This is the likeness of God.

A man who does not rule over his spirit is like a city broken down (Proverbs 25:28 It is a calamity of man if he does not govern his spirit in the likeness of God. Some people set aside time for prayer, worship, and meditation. But many they have no control over their spirit. The soul is not in the likeness of God if it abandons the spirit without control. The greatest sin is distorting God's likeness in man. Just as the Holy Spirit performs the will of God the Father rather than the will of Jesus Christ, the spirit of man must do the will of the soul rather than the will of the flesh. This is the likeness of God. On the day Adam was formed, his divine likeness seal appeared exactly in th likeness of God.

Adam Damaged The Second Major Seal

The second sin of Adam: When Adam sinned; the Spirit of Adam began to serve the will of the body rather than the will of the soul. The Spirit of Adam did not act according to the likeness of God. The reason for this is because the flesh of man made the spirit his slave. Thus, on the day of sin, Adam's spirit and flesh did not behave in the likeness of God, but rather destroyed the likeness of God in him. Adam, in the conclusion, destroyed the second seal of God in him.

Important Note:

We learned in the previous lesson that the atom was created with the sign of God. Breaking this divine sign within the atom leads to massive destruction through the emission of gamma rays. This raises an important question: if the sign of God within human beings is broken, would a similar destructive force be released to bring ruin upon humanity?

The answer is yes. Humanity itself emits a hidden, dangerous force that works against its own survival. This invisible destroyer is already impacting lives in destructive ways, though it often remains concealed from human awareness. In the upcoming lessons we will learn how the destruction of God's seal in man has destructive impact on his existence.

THE INVISIBLE MONARCH

The Birth Of Conscience

Conscience allows us to do two things:

Pass judgment on ourselves;

approve or condemn our own conduct

-Edwin Louis Cole

When a person consumes spicy food, bodily fluid rapidly fills his eyes and nose. It is natural. Similarly, if someone kills another; the law will instantly step in to judge that individual. This is also natural. When Adam broke the divine seal in him, "the destroyer" colonized to him and began to govern and destroy him naturally. So there is no reason for God to punish man. The "destroyer" in man destroys man. This man-born "destroyer" ruthlessly dominated the man, torturing and killing him till the end. We will explore this mystery further by the end of this chapter.

Do you know what the most challenging question for biologists is? "Where did man's conscience come from?." Those who believe in evolution cannot answer this question. Even philosophers, scientists, and many religious teachings have no answer to this topic. In this lesson, we shall vividly comprehend where this mysterious conscience originated from and why it is so crucial in governing man's existence.

Everyone has a basic expectation to know what was in the fruit that Adam and Eve ate. God noticed that everything he had created was in order and good. Thus, the Garden of Eden was in order and good. He produced several types of lovely and excellent trees. God created the Tree of Life. He also created the Tree of knowing good and evil. Do you know the uniqueness of the fruit of the tree of knowing good and evil? Do you know the effect of eating this fruit? If anyone eats this fruit, the knowledge of knowing what is good and what is evil will be born in them.

Genesis 2:9 And out of the ground made the LORD God to grow every tree that is pleasant to the sight, and good for food; the tree of life also in the midst of the garden, and the tree of knowledge of good and evil.

If you eat the fruit of the tree of knowing good and evil, it will continue to give you knowledge of what is good and evil. You may ask: What's wrong with knowing what's good and evil, and why should God forbid such fruit? I've provided answers to these questions below. Do you understand what conscience is? A person's conscience is their moral sense of understanding what is right and wrong. The conscience is an inner voice in every individual that tells him what is right and evil in his life. You could feel that you have been told from inside, "this is good, that is evil, you should do it, and you should not do it". This is the conscience. It is residing within all men.

Before eating this fruit, Adam was unaware of what is good and evil. Since beginning, God's Spirit was the one who told Adam what was good and what was evil. Adam was led by God's Spirit. The Bible says, "For as many as are led by the Spirit of God, these are sons of God" (Romans 8:14). Surely, Adam was son of God. As a result, Adam and Eve lacked a conscience that could tell them what was good and what was evil. Adam and Eve got the conscience of knowing good and evil when they ate the fruit of that tree, which was knowing good and evil. Who are the parents of conscience? The conscience's parent is the tree of knowing good and evil.

When Adam and Eve ate this fruit, they received a conscience capable of knowing good and evil. In the next paragraphs, we will see how conscience became the fundamental tool for all human suffering, and how conscience altered mankind. Some may wonder how consuming the fruit of knowledge of good and evil may invite conscience in Adam. Continue to read till the end, you can trace out more evidences for the migration of conscience.

Conclusion: The first man received conscience that could speak good and evil after eating the fruit of the tree of knowledge, knowing good and evil.

The Flawless Court

Courage without conscience is a wild beast

- Robert Green Ingersoll

There is a higher court than courts of justice
and that is the court of conscience.
It supercedes all other courts
- Mahatma Gandhi

O conscience, upright and stainless,
how bitter a sting to thee is a little fault!
- Dante Alighieri

The subject of conscience frequently confounds psychologists and theologians. This appears to them to be a mystery. We can surely tell if a man is guilty of sin or innocent because of his conscience. Crimes undetected by the criminal courts are focused on the conscience. Even though a false witness invalidates a man's crimes in the courts, the guilty of sin is always there in man's conscience. The constitution of the government creates the world's courts. However, God established a special court in each of us known as conscience. This is greater than all of the world's courts. Even if no one finds the fault to blame, the own conscience of man knows the faults. Conscience can blame without tolerance. It is the conscience that prevails above all courts of the world. Only the conscience can point out even minor errors of an individual. A man can deceive his parents, teachers, master, relatives, friends, husband, wife, and even spouse. But no one can deceive their own conscience. The conscience can record, even small mistakes without error. No one can escape from the conscience. Holidays are declared to all courts in the world. But only one court works without any holiday that is conscience. There may be several errors in man-made courts. But conscience is the only court that operates without error.

Romans 2:15 Which shew the work of the law written in their hearts, their conscience also bearing witness, and their thoughts the mean while accusing or else excusing one another;

Almost all the legal systems of every nation are now framed based on conscience and thus, the world is ruled by the conscience. Conscience is in a powerful position to dominate the world. There is conscience in the Arts, there is conscience in literature, there is conscience in philosophy, there is conscience in history, there is conscience in science, there is conscience in medicine, there is conscience in doing good, there is conscience in love, there is conscience at death, there is conscience in taking care of children and women, there is conscience in charity, and there is conscience in thief too. thus, conscience is filled everywhere and it leads every man and also the world. Making good people and a good society is the prime work of the conscience.

The Enslaver

The person that loses their conscience

has nothing left worth keeping

- Izaak Walton

Sin in the conscience, is like Jonah in a ship,
which causeth such a tempest,
that the conscience is like a troubled sea,
whose waters cannot rest,
or it is like a mote in the eye,
which causeth a perpetual trouble while it is there
-Thomas Brooks

Oh, Conscience! Conscience! man's most faithful friend,
Him canst thou comfort, ease, relieve, defend;
But if he will thy friendly checks forego,
Thou art, oh! woe for me, his deadliest foe!
-George Crabbe, Struggles of Conscience

Those who offend the voice of the court of conscience have produced the most catastrophic repercussions. Hitler, a dictator, lived in rebellion of conscience. Take a look at what Hitler stated about conscience. In his Conversations with Hermann Rauschning, president of the senate of the Free City of Danzig (Gdansk) in 1933 and 1934, Hitler said to him:

"I liberate man from the constraint of a spirit…(and) from the filthy and degrading torments inflicted on himself by a chimera called conscience and morality, and from the claims of a freedom and personal autonomy that only very few can ever be up to"

According to this statement, Hitler believed in freedom from conscience as the next logical step rather than freedom of conscience.

Because Hitler acted against his conscience, he killed more than six million Jews unconscionably. He killed mercilessly, from babies to stagnant old men. Not only that, Hitler was the most important reason for the outbreak of World War II. World War II which was started by Hitler was the most horrific war in world history. About 70 million to 85 million people died in this world war. And also about 3 percent of the world population was wiped out by this war. About 20 million to 30 million people have died of war-related poverty and pestilences. The German government has issued a statement that about 7.3 million and ninety-five thousand people died in Germany alone. Around 27 million individuals were murdered in the Soviet Union alone, including 8.7 million troops and 10.9 million civilians.The death roar was rocking the earth, and time had stopped. The original cause of all of this was Hitler. This happened because he disobeyed his conscience. The result of antagonism to conscience has impacted the whole planet. Many people believed that Hitler was the personification of evil. But what actually happened? Because he despised his own conscience and acted against it, the world could not endure the repercussions, and he died by suicide in retaliation for his own conscience. Through Hitler, the world learned that those who insulted the court of conscience had to pay a hefty price.

The Supreme Ruler

Conscience is the authentic voice of God to you

- Rutherford B. Hayes

Dangerous consequences will follow when politicians and rulers forget moral principles - Dalai Lama

Following World War II, which Hitler started, nations throughout the world became conscious of the law of conscience. The world realised that anyone who goes against their conscience would ruin themselves as well as all they achieved. Recognizing this truth of conscience, international governments established more conscience-based legislation. The United Nations urges that each country's legislation be guided by conscience. Every year on April 5th, the United Nations declares a "International Day of Conscience." It is a crucial aspect of human life.

The significance of "International Conscience Day" is that everyone should listen to their conscience for personal peace as well as global peace. Mutual friendship was developed among countries after the founding of the United Nations on the basis of conscience. The world's population began to grow. If somebody stands up for conscience, the conscience will stand up for them. Anyone who goes against their conscience will be destroyed by it, and no one can bear its punishments. God had cautioned Adam not to eat the fruit of the tree of the knowing good and evil, knowing that such a dreadful conscience would be created and devastate mankind. All people today are suffering as a result of Adam's failure to listen to God. People are trapped in the horror of conscience.

In this world, there are people who defame the law. There are plenty of fake witnesses in the courtroom. There are people who deceive the judiciary with their false testimony to convert the unjust to justice and justice to injustice. But no one can deceive the court of conscience. The testimony of conscience can put sinners to death. There is no one who could speak against their own conscience and overcome it. Because of the domination of the various consciousness of the world, there are many people who have forgotten their conscience. But when a man dies, his conscience that was ignored will arise against his soul. The guilty conscience will witness against him. No one can escape from the matrix of conscience at all.

According to several religions, everyone has a book where they have account of their sins. Nobody has ever seen such a book. However, no one can deny the existence of the book of conscience, which all religious people are aware of and which justifies every sin. Every man was given this book by God. Your conscience and your court are where you make the choice to send your soul to either immortality or destruction. Every action that a person takes against their conscience is continuously recorded by their conscience. Every man and woman's conscience will be audible on the Day of Judgment. The conscience will throw evil men and evil women who were acting as if they are good into the terrible prison of a guilty conscience! No one can escape from conscience!

Conclusion: Conscience makes laws. These laws govern the individual, society, and the world. The deeds of those who disobeyed the law were judged by conscience. It will judge like a faithful and righteous judge, and then it will throw disobeyed into terrible prison. People can escape from anything in the world, but no one can escape from the court of conscience.

The Deadly Nagger

And I know of the future judgment
How dreadful so'er it be
That to sit alone with my conscience
Would be judgment enough for me

- *Charles William Stubbs, Alone with my conscience*

The first and greatest punishment of the sinner is the conscience of sin - Lucius Annaeus Seneca

The torture of an evil conscience is the hell of a living soul- John Calvin

The conscience is the only one that establishes the best and most accurate laws in the world. Similarly, conscience is adamant in perpetuating those laws. You may think that conscience is the best one to instruct us on what is good or what is evil. But the conscience does not stop by saying what is good and what is evil. It goes beyond that. If someone does something against the conscience, the conscience will immediately rage up against that man. For example, suppose someone is walking down the street, looking at something, and he thinks he should steal it somehow. "Do not steal," the conscience says. If the substance is stolen beyond the law of the conscience, the conscience shall record his transgression as a crime against him. The guilty conscience would keep nagging him "you have stolen ... you have stolen ...". The conscience of vengeance for that sin will keep on raging. Do you understand now why God said that the fruit of the tree of knowing good and evil should not be eaten? The conscience will record the sin against him. God knew very well that sin would kill him. So God told him not to eat such a fruit.

Genesis 2:17 But of the tree of the knowledge of good and evil, thou shalt not eat of it: for in the day that thou eatest thereof thou shalt surely die.

When Adam and Eve ate this fruit, they gained a conscience. Adam and Eve were guilty in their own views. This is how the conscience originated. This conscience was bothering them by reminding them of their transgression. This nagging turned out to be the poison that killed them. God advised Adam not to eat the fruit, knowing that if he eats, he would die the same day. Their conscience's poison killed them both.

Conclusion: The conscience which was colonized in the first man became a poison to kill him.

❖

THE DEAD-KARMA

You are free to choose, but you are not free from the consequence of your choice - Author Unknown

Conscience is the perfect interpreter of life - Karl Barth

If anyone has a conscience it's generally a guilty one - Max Frisch

Karma surrounds us in a mysterious way that no one understands. This is why many people are still perplexed about karma. Some spiritual leaders tell people to keep their mouths shut, claiming, "Karma is just the result of one's deeds. That's all! thus, no one should have any doubts regarding karma." But, as for karma, why do people say,

""What the heck is this?"

"Karma is after me."

"Karma has caught up with him."

"Everyone must bear their own karma."

"When am I going to be free of this karma?"

"The karma of Satan"

"Everyone's karma follows him." Etc.,

The Meaning Of Karma

There is conscience within every human being that conscience keeps telling people what is good and what is evil. It is the conscience that enacts the laws of what to do and what not to do. A man works in accordance with the law of conscience or against the law of conscience. Good work or evil work completed pivoting conscience is called karma.

Karma can be divided into two types as Real Time Karma and Dead-Karma.

a). If anyone is currently doing work, it is "real-time karma". This is the first type of Karma.

b). When a person completed work, it is finished work. That particular work (karma) is not going to come back. Therefore, this dead work can be termed "Dead-Karma". This is the second type of Karma.

3. Real-time karma can be divided into "real time-good - karma" and "real time-evil-karma".

a). If one does exactly what the conscience says, it is called "real time-good-karma"

b). If one does what is against the conscience, it is called "real-time–evil -karma"

***

Dead-Karma can be divided into two types as below.

a). When someone completed the work (karma) exactly what the conscience said, it is "dead-good-karma".

b). When someone completed the work (karma) against what the conscience said, it is "dead-evil-karma". We call this dead-evil-karma a "sin".

Conscience not only enacts the law, but it also serves as "man's inner court," much as a nation's tribunal focuses on the crimes of the convicted in a court. So, when a person has completed a task, the "dead-good-karma" and "dead-evil-karma" remain in the court of conscience. They are deeply embedded in the conscience.

In Hebrews 9:14, the word "Dead-Works" which is in conscience is translated as "Nirjiva Karma" in some Indian languages. It means "Dead-karma". Dead-Karma and Dead works have the same meaning.

Nobody cares about dead-good-karma. If the government enacts laws to follow, everyone must comply with the laws. No one should violate this. Does any nation give a gift to a person stating "you are a good citizen" in appreciation of citizens who strictly follow the laws? Not at all! It is the duty of every citizen to respect the laws of the constitution of the country. Similarly, it is the duty of every individual to respect the laws of their own conscience. Therefore, when a person does good things in accordance with his own conscience, he should not expect appreciation from his conscience. He must continuously repeat the good works as per conscience. Look at how cruel! This is part of the conscience. On the Day of Judgment, the dead-good- karma is there in the conscience as though it were not. You will understand the reason for this in the coming passages.

Dead-evil-karma stays in the conscience strongly. This type of karma is very cruel. If something is done against the conscience, that dead-evil-karma will not keep quiet. The dead-evil-karma is alive to take revenge. It causes great pains to humans. We will see in the next section about the terrible consequences of dead-evil-karma.

This is how spiritualists must classify karma and teach people. People should no longer say just karma, but should people say, "what the heck it is, karma chasing me away, he is caught with karma, let everyone should suffer their karma, what the karma did, when will I be free from this karma?, Saturn's karma, each one's karma will follow him". Karma is work but it is not only work, karma needed to be classified as above for better understanding.

Conclusion: Karma is nothing but work. The finished work is called Dead-Karma. There are two types of Dead-Karma. If someone has finished good work, it is called dead-good-karma. In the court of conscience, the dead-good- karma is there as though it were not. If someone has finished evil work, it is called dead-evil-karma. This dead-evil-karma is willfully glued to the conscience as sin. Every man's sin is in the court of his own conscience. The evil-Dead-Karma is so terrible.

Conscience To Dead-Karma

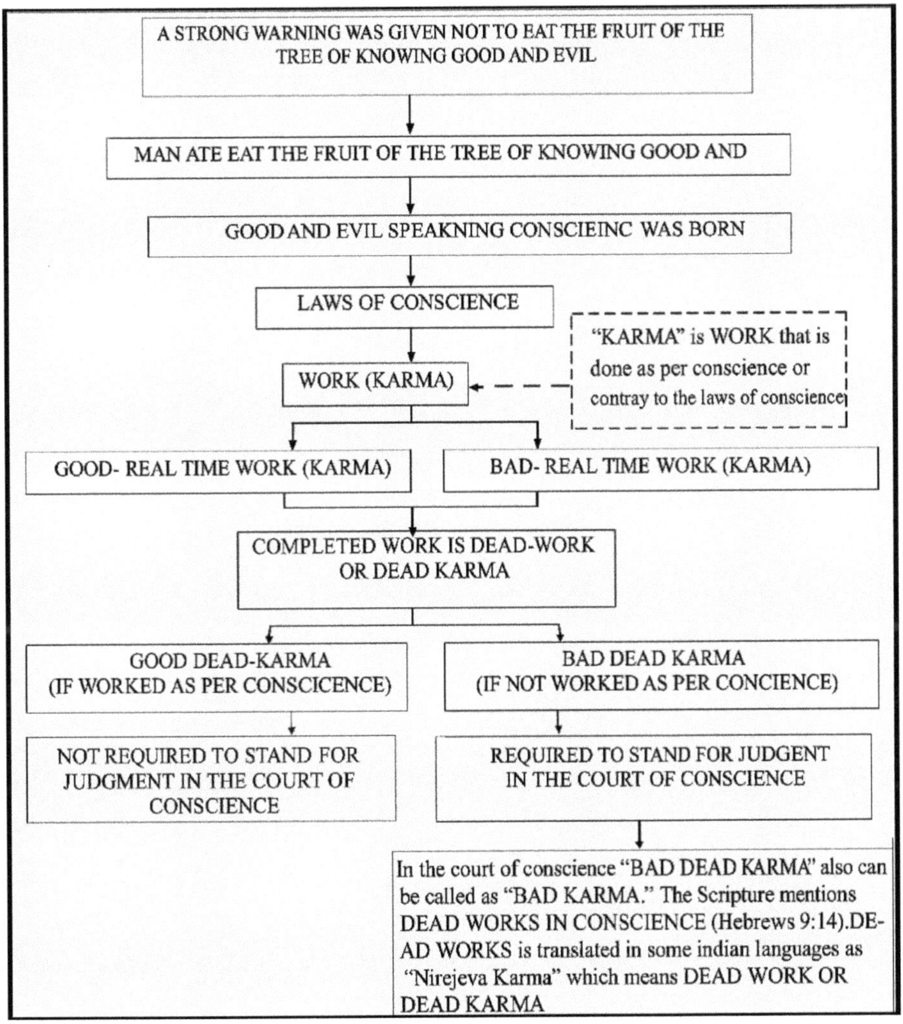

DEAD-KARMA: EVERY ACTION HAS UNEQUAL REACTION

My conscience hath a thousand several tongues,

And every tongue brings in a several tale,

And every tale condemns me for a villain

William Shakespeare, Richard III (c. 1591),

Act V, scene 3, line 193

According to Newton's law, every action has an equal and opposite reaction. According to the book Aghora III: The Law of Karma, karma is the same as Newton's law. Because no religious book implies there is just one equal punishment for one lying or any other sin, I believe this book's (Aghora III: The Law of Karma) assertion is incorrect. According to numerous religious texts, if one person kills another, he may be punished on Earth. Even if a murderer is punished and murdered on Earth, the murderer must continue to suffer several times in hell for the same offence. This is the law of karma. Karma's law cannot be identical to Newton's law. The "Dead-Karma" that exists in the conscience of every human being is dreadful. Its effects will build up like the foul smell of a corpse. Even if only one dead body decompose, the foul smell will accumulate as if 10 million corpses are decomposing. The stink is indescribable. This is the outcome of a decomposing corpse. Similarly, every man's "Dead-Karma" will have disastrous results. It is unbearable. Karma surrounds man's knowledge, Karma surrounds man's wisdom, Karma surrounds man's energy, Karma surrounds man's work, Karma surrounds man's wealth, Karma surrounds man's memories, Karma envelops human behaviours, Karma surrounds man's birth, and Karma surrounds man's death. And the list goes on and on. There is no limit to the horror of dead-karma. In the grip of the Dead-Karma, man's life is pitiful. All of man's current woes are the result of Dead-Karma (sin). The man who thinks about the consequences of karma will be damn tired. There are so many dreadful consequences that humans cannot tolerate.

Conscience records the sins of man's spirit, soul, and body. Nobody can delete these records. For dead-karma, conscience has the scream of vengeance in its court. No one could control Dead-karma. Dead-karma of man's sins, spirit, soul, and body, are tightly gripped in the conscience.The horror of sin (dead-karma)is so great. It will parade its deadly authority until hell.

Horror Of Dead-Karma On Earth

According to Christianity, Judaism, Islam, Hinduism, and Buddhism, the Dead-works follow everyone without fail. And everyone must receive the effects of the dead-works. Let us examine what the religions say about this in depth.

1). Judaism: "Whatever man sows will reap the same" says Judaism

Job 4:8 ...they that plow iniquity, and sow wickedness, reap the same.

Hosea 10:13 Ye have plowed wickedness, ye have reaped iniquity; ye have eaten the fruit of lies: because thou didst trust in thy way, in the multitude of thy mighty men.

Proverbs 22:8 He that soweth iniquity shall reap vanity: and the rod of his anger shall fail.

2). Islam: "Whatever man sows will reap the same" says Islam

Quran 2:141 (Yusuf Ali translation) ...They shall reap the fruit of what they did and ye of what ye do! Of their merits there is no question in your case.

3). Hinduism: "Whatever man sows will reap the same" says Hinduism

But with whatever disposition of mind (a man) forms any act, he reaps its result. (Hindu, Laws of Manu chapter 7)

And as is his desire, so is his will; and as is his will, so is his deed; and whatever deed he does, that he will reap.(Hindu, Upanishads vol. 2, Brihadaranyaka-Upanishad Part 3)

4). Buddhism: "Man cannot escape from his evil works" says Buddhism

Not in the sky, nor in the depths of the sea, nor hiding in the cleft of the rocks, there is no place on earth where one can take one's stand to escape from an evil deed. (Buddhist, Dhammapada – Sayings of the Buddha 1 (tr. J. Richards)

5). Christianity: "Whatever man sows will reap the same" says Christianity

2 Corinthians 9:6 But this I say, He which soweth sparingly shall reap also sparingly; and he which soweth bountifully shall reap also bountifully.

Galatians 6:7-8 Be not deceived; God is not mocked: for whatsoever a man soweth, that shall he also reap. For he that soweth to his flesh shall of the flesh reap corruption; but he that soweth to the Spirit shall of the Spirit reap life everlasting.

Every religion teaches that man will be rewarded for his actions. Even in hell, the soul of man will suffer the consequences of all dead works.

Horror Of Dead-Karma In Hell

Islam's Concept of hell:

In Islam, if a lady reveals her hair to a stranger, she will suffer forever in hell, without rest or end.

1. There is continuous burning fire for renegades
2. There is continuous a torturing place for witches and fortunetellers
3. There is continuous a torturing furnace for the disbelievers
4. There is continuous a torturing bottomless abyss for hypocrites

Muhammad, Buraq and Gabriel observe "shameless women" being contineouly punished in Hell for prostitution

Hinduism's Concept of hell

Various punishments in hell are mentioned Garuda Purana, Bhagavatap Purana and Vishnupurana of the Hindu religion as follows:

1. Tamisram (Heavy flogging): If anyone deceives the materials of others will be thrown into Tamisram hell. In this gloomy hell, sinners will be tied to ropes and made to starve without water and food.
2. Andhatamtrsam (Flogging): Those who cheat others and enjoy other's wife or their children for self pleasure will be blinded by stabbing their eyes. And they will be thrown into the dark Andhatamtrsam Hell.
3. Rauravam (torment by snakes): Selfish people and those who destroy their families will be punished by serpents in Rauravam hell.
4. Mahararuravam (death by snakes): Those who unjustly destroy others' property or posses others property will be tortured by serpents in the Mahararuravam hell.
5. Kumbhipakam (cooking by oil): Those who kill the animals for their pleasure will be roasted in the boiling oil of Kumbpakam hell.
6. Kalasutram (burning in hell): Those who do not respect the elders, and those who torment their parents will be punished in a fiery hell called Kalasutram.
7. Asitapatram (sharp flogging): Those who speak against God and disrespect religious beliefs without doing their job properly will be left in hell called Asitapatram and there they will be continued to be pierced with ghostly weapons.
8. Sukaramukham (Crushed and tormented): Those who misuse their positions, bully others, and unjustly punish innocent people will be

crushed by the giants in Sukaramukham Hell, and also will continue to be chewed by the teeth of terrible animals.

9. Andhakupam (Attack of the animals): People having capability to help others but not helping, discouraging, oppressing, threatening, and spoiling good works will be thrown into andhakupam hell. There, they will be pushed into the wells to be bruised and eaten by the beasts like lion, tiger, donkey, eagle, snake, scorpion etc.
10. Taptamurti (Burning Alive): Those who do steal and robber will be roasted in the fire of Taptamurti hell.
11. Krimibhojanam (eaten by worms): Those who dishonoring guests, using others for their own benefit, and using the hard work of others for their own goodness will be sent to hell, where the worms, insects, and serpents will continue to devour their souls and bodies.
12. Salmali (torturing images): The lustful and the fornicators will be sent to Salmali hell, where they will be pierced with red hot wrought iron rods into their genital organs.
13. Vajjirakantakasali: Those who commit adultery with animals and forcible prostitutes with human beings will be sent to Vajjirakantakasali hell, where they are pierced with sharp diamond needles while they are embrace fire-breathing poles.
14. Vaitarani (River of Filth): Vaitarani is a hell for people with power rabid, masking, and hypocrisy. This hell is full of impurities like man's feces, urine, blood, hair, bones, claws and rotten flesh. These sinners will be repeatedly crushed there.
15. Puyodakam (Well of hell): Puyodakam is a hell for the sinners who do not marry the woman but turn her prostitute and enjoy her like a

beast. These sinners will be punished by the poisonous creatures in this hell which will be full of man's feces, urine, blood and saliva.

16. Pranarotham: Those who torture the animals and kill them for food will be thrown into hell called Pranarotham.
17. Visasanam: It is the hell of the rich who can only brag about themselves without helping the poor. They will be beaten constantly in this hell.
18. Lalabakhsam: Lalabaksham is a hell for those who commit forceful ugly adultery with their spouse or husband. Here such people will be constantly tortured to drink the filthy fluid.
19. Sarmayasana: Looters, food poisoners, house burners, and assassins will be thrown into a hell-filled with rabid dogs and tortured there.
20. Aveis Hell: False witnesses, liars, false promisers, and producers of false evidences will be thrown into the deep shallows of Avies hell, where they will be drowned into the dust.
21. Aiyaapanam: Men who drink alcohol and drink dirty beverages will be punished by compelling them to drink the flames of valcano, and women will be forced to drink molten iron.
22. Raksopjaxam: Those who torture and kill animals, sacrifice human beings, and eat their flesh will be thrown into the Rakshobjaxam hell; there they will be bitten by animals. There will be weeping and crying.
23. Sulayotram: people who are involved in Suicide, deception, murder and betrayal will be thrown into the sharp knife jungles of hell called Sulaprotham. There their bodies will be hanged on sharp knifes.

24. Ksharagardam Hell: Those who are involved in insulting good people, doing evil deeds, spoiling the name of the elderly, living in pride, and bragging, will be hanged after stabbing on living organs.
25. Tandasugam: Those who use others as beasts and torture them will be bitten and eaten little by little in hell called tandasugam.
26. Varadotham: Those who persecute animals that live on mountains and forests will have their hands tied up in the hell called Varadhotam and will be attacked with poison, fire and various other weapons.
27. Paryavarthanam: Crows and eagles will kill the sinners who humiliate the abandoned in the hell called Paryavarthanam, by feeding them to the hungry crows and eagles.
28. Susimukam: Those who are not doing good works but add wealth by illegally earning and hoarding will be tormented by stabbing all over their body in the hell called Susimugam.

The punishments given for sinners in these hells are cruel and endless. This is how the Hinduism says that karma is restless and vengeful.

The Concept of hell in Christianity: In Christianity, we read in the Holy Bible that the sinful people will be tormented in hell's fire, and the fire that punishes them will never cease.

Mar 9:43-44 And if thy hand offend thee, cut it off: it is better for thee to enter into life maimed, than having two hands to go into hell, into the fire that never shall be quenched: Where their worm dieth not, and the fire is not quenched.

Buddhism's Concept of hell: In Buddhism, there are eighteen different types of hell. According to Buddhism, every man must suffer in hell for his sins. Some of the sins and hells allocated to sinners are listed here.

1. Hell to tear tongues: This hell is assigned to tear the tongue gosippers

2. Hell of Blades: The Hell of Blades is allotted to those who wreck others' marriages.

3. Hell of Blades: The Hell of Blades is allotted to those who wreck others' marriages.

4. Self-image Hell: Those who avoid punishment on Earth are consigned to self-image hell.

5. Steam Hell: Hypocrites and rebels are sent to Steam Hell.

6. Molten copper hell: This is the punishment for those who seek vengeance.

7. Mountaineering Hell with Blades: Those who kill dumb creatures for their own enjoyment are assigned to a sharp sword hell.

8. Naked Ice Hell: This is the punishment for conspirators, racists, and adulterers.

9. Hell cooked in oil: Hell fried in oil is reserved for prostitutes, thieves, and criminals.

10. Hell for bullying animals: This hellfire is reserved for individuals who mistreat animals.

11. The Torment of Carrying Rocks: This hell is allocated to people who forsake their children and are forced to carry large rocks through unclean water.

12. Feeding by ghosts: Those who waste food are destined to this hell. Sinners will be nourished by ghosts in this hell

13. Soaking in blood: Those who have no regard for others will be saturated in blood in this inferno.

14. Suicidal Hell: This hell is reserved for individuals who commit suicide.

13. Soaking in blood: In this hell, those who have no respect for others will be soaked in the blood.

14. Repeated Suiciding Hell: This hell is assigned for those who commit suicide. Here the sinners will be wandering day and night in the air of anxiety and heavy rains; and repeatedly they will be forced to commit suicide.

15. Hell to tear: The tomb riders will be torn into pieces in this hell repeatedly.

16. Volcanic Hell: A yellowish fiery hell is assigned for thieves and robbers.

17. Hell of grinding mill: This hell is assigned to the oppressors of the weak.

18. Cutting piece by piece Hell: This hell is assigned to those who use loopholes in the law and sin. They will be repeatedly cut into pieces in this hell.

In Buddhism, there are eighteen various types of hell, as described above. The culprits must pay the price. According to Buddhism, no sinners will be exempt from these hells.

Jainism's Concept of hell: According to Jainism, there are seven hells. They are:

1. Ratnaprabha

2. Valukaprabha
3. Pankaprabha
4. Tamahaprabha
5. Mahatamahaprabha
6. Dhumaprabha
7. Sharkaraprabha

Christianity and Judaism's Concept of hell: In Christianity and Judaism, the Dead-Karma (sins) stays in man. According to Proverbs 6:16-19, a proud look, a lying tongue, and hands that shed innocent blood, a heart that deviseth wicked imaginations, feet that be swift in running to mischief, a false witness that speaketh lies, and he that soweth discord among brethren. As per Galatians 5:19-21 Adultery, fornication, uncleanness, Idolatry, lascivious- ness, witchcraft, hatred, variance, emulations, wrath, strife, seditions, heresies, Envyings, murders, drunkenness, revellings, etc., What more is sin? creating gods other than the one God who created the heavens and the earth, worshiping such God, not loving God, blasphemy against God, unforgiveness, murder, adultery, fornication, lying, not observing sabbath, forgetting goodness of God, disrespecting father and mother, robbery, false witness, coveting another man's wife, coveting neighbor's house, coveting neighbor's farm, coveting neighbor's cattle, nor anything that is his!, If you know how to do good but if do not do that, it is sin. Giving to interest, not helping, not loving neighbors, bribery and greed are sins.

According to Mahatma Gandhi, the father of India, "Wealth without Work, pleasure without conscience, knowledge without character, commerce (Business) without morality (Ethics), science without humanity, religion without sacrifice, and politics without principle" are sins. Like this, we can keep on listing out about Dead-Karma (sin) in man. Every dead-karma has terrible consequences. Sinners will be put into the fire. Their fire will never be ceased, and their worm will never die.

Conscience will revenge the individual who has dead-evil-karma. As a result, the man must be punished. Karma's vengeance does not end with physical death, even if a person is punished and slain on Earth. Karma is a cruelty that flies up to hell. That is why all sinners are perpetually punished in hell.

Conclusion: All Faiths Have Similar View On The Punishments Of Sin

Every person in this world is a sinner. Nobody is without sin. All faiths teach that man must pay for his misdeeds! So, what is the path to freedom? The laws of the court of conscience must be followed by everyone, from the monarch to the servant. God created the court of conscience in each individual. God has always desired to remove the lethal poison known as Dead-Karma from man and restore the Divine seal. But there was a significant obstacle to not doing it. The barrier was the accumulating offences before the court of conscience. All Dead-Karma returns to seek vengeance. Those crimes will not be forgotten unless vengeance is imposed. Vengeance was extremely terrible; it is not as equal as the crime.

First, the guilty person must be punished in the flesh, and then must be killed in the same fleshly body. When someone dies, the Dead-Karma will drag the soul to hell. And then, the soul must continue to be punished in hell without ceasing. Finally, the soul must be killed there. It will be the most horrorful death. If everyone is punished this way, nobody will be spared. The mankind is in great trouble. All the trials of men were failed as mentioned in the upcoming section. There was nothing could be done to free man.

WHEN THE WORLD FAILS

And I know of the future judgment

How dreadful so'er it be

That to sit alone with my conscience

Would be judgment enough for me.

(Charles William Stubbs, Alone with my conscience)

***

Worship without sacrifice is a sin-Mahatma Gandhi

In world history, animals were sacrificed by various religious people to their respective gods to get rid of Dead-Karma (dead work). When such sacrifices were offered, the people believed that the anger of the gods for the sin of mankind would be covered that god would make peace with the people of that particular religion. This is how billions of people have sacrificed animals for thousands of years. Some religions now say that we are not offering sacrifices. But who can deny the sacrifices now made before our very eyes; and the sacrifices made in the past? Who told humans to make such sacrifices? Is it god or is it the conscience of people? Whatever it is, we all come to know that animal sacrifice was done to temporarily prevent the effects of dead work which are in the conscience.

Egyptian animal sacrifice: It is well known that the cultures and traditions of the Egyptians were the forerunners of all religious cultures and practices in the world. According to history, The Ancient Egyptians settled themselves on the narrow strip of alluvial soil along both banks of the Nile about 7000 years ago. Although the cultures and rituals of the ancient Egyptians were the oldest of all religious cultures and customs, they were no longer popular like many other cultures, because only less people talk about this culture and liturgical traditions. The people of Egypt offered animal sacrifices to their gods. Even human beings are sacrificed for the welfare of the nation and their masters. The sole purpose of these sacrifices was to that god would bless the people when they offer sacrifices for sins against god. Whenever the people of Egypt died, some sacrifice was made on the side of their dead bodies. The Egyptians believed that such a sacrifice would cover their sins.

Mesopotamian animal sacrifice: Sacrifices were common in the Mesopotamian kingdoms. It was important for them to offer sacrifices to their gods in the main liturgy.

Grecian animal sacrifice: In ancient Greek liturgy, after sacrificing the domestic animals on the altar, people would sing and pray. The altar was built outside the temple. This altar was not associated with the temple. Their principle is that the sacrificial animal must be perfect. The sacrificial animal was decorated with garlands and marched to the altar. A woman would hold a hidden knife in hand and run the procession. After many rituals, the sacrificial animal was sacrificed on the altar. When the animal fell, there was a cry. Women must cry out loud to mark the sacrifice. Then the people would take the blood and pour it on the altar. The Greeks sacrificed bulls, cows, goats, sheep, and pigs. Sometimes they even sacrificed horses and donkeys. These Greek rituals are said to have played an important role in restoring the broken relationship between humans and god.

Roman animal sacrifice: Animal sacrifices to the gods were the ancient Romans' most effective form of worship. The Romans typically offered up goats and pigs as sacrifices. Animals that had been purified were sacrificed. They garlanded the sacrificing animals. The horns of the cows, which are sacrificed, were gold-plated. Such creatures are sacrificed in front of their gods. The Romans adopted many of the religious ceremonies and practices of the Greeks. The Greek gods were also embraced as Roman deities. It is believed that the sacrifice practices of the Romans had a significant impact on how people and how people interacted with their deity.

Animal sacrifice in Islam: There are sacrifices in Islam as well. In Islam, Eid al-Adha is known as the Festival of Sacrifice. This is the second-largest festival of Islam. It is special to offer sacrifices at this festival. Nearly one million animals were sacrificed in Indonesia in 2014 alone. About 2.5 million animals including goats, sheep, cows, and camels were sacrificed every year in Turkey. And about ten million animals are sacrificed in Pakistan every year. Likewise, goats, sheep, cows, and camels are sacrificed in Saudi Arabia.

The Arabic word for sacrifice is Qurbanī (Arabic: قربانى). The Hebrew word Qurban (qorbān - sacrifice) and the Syrian word "Qurbana" (qurbānā - sacrifice) are having the same meaning. This word refers to the Qurbanī which means sacrifice performed during the festival of Baqrid. Muslims say that the meaning of the word is "bring someone to come close to the Lord by means of sacrifice." The sacrifice was used to remove the barriers between god and human beings.

According to the dictates of Islam, Muslims, all over the world are obliged to sacrifice unblemished sheep, goats, cows, or camels. The town of Mina, near the Islamic pilgrimage site of Mecca, has special places to sacrifice animals.

Animal sacrifice in ancient Hinduism: According to history, because so many animals were being offered as sacrifices to the Greek gods, following the death of Alexander the Great the Greeks thought about ceasing the animal sacrifice. Since then, offering animals as sacrifices to Greek gods has become rare. Hinduism places a high value on sacrifices and offerings. You may have heard about the shocking tragedy that occurred in Nepal in 2009 when over 2.5 million livestock were killed to Hindu gods, shocking the entire globe. Nepal is a Hindu country. Pictures of these sacrifices are shown here. Despite furious protests against animal sacrifices at the Hindu holiday of Gadhimai in 2014, more than one lakh animals were sacrificed in Nepal.

Cow sacrifices were performed in Nepal in 2018 in honour of Hindu deities. Only once a year does the public get access to the temple. One of the biggest Hindu festivals in Nepal is Dashein. This celebration honours the goddess Durga, reflecting both Nepal's devotion to her and her ancient rituals. In India, sacrifices are still done for Hindu gods. Hindus believe that offering an animal as sacrifice can atone for their sins and bring them closer to God.

Animal sacrifice in Judaism: The sacrifice made to God is known as "Qurban" in Judaism and Islam (Hebrew: קָרְבָּן qārbān; Arabic: قربان).. The burned offering, the sin offering, and the guilt offering were offered by the Jews (Israelites) to God. They must make sacrifices in order to atone for their sins, according to the Israelites' holy text. Jews offered up bulls, goats, and lambs as sacrifices. They offered animal sacrifices in their temple from the time of Moses until the fall of the second temple. According to the Israelites' religious text, after these offerings, Israel's iniquity was covered up and God's glory descended upon the temple. These offerings were offered in order to save the human soul. These sacrifices were offered to cover the evil-dead-works in the conscience.

Samaritan animal sacrifice: Moses instructed the Israelites to bless Mount Gerizim when they entered Canaan.

> *Deuteronomy 11:29-30 And it shall come to pass, when the LORD thy God hath brought thee in unto the land whither thou goest to possess it, that thou shalt put the blessing upon mount Gerizim, and the curse upon mount Ebal. Are they not on the other side Jordan, by the way where the sun goeth down, in the land of the Canaanites, which dwell in the champaign over against Gilgal, beside the plains of Moreh?*

The Samaritan woman had been talking to Jesus about this mountain (John 4: 21–24). On this Mount Gerizim, on April 29, 2018, the Samaritans offered goats and sheep as sacrifices for the Passover holiday. The Samaritans made sacrifices of animals as atonement for sin and wickedness. The Samaritans' sacred text makes it very clear that they must make sacrifices in order to atone for sin.

Canaanites animal sacrifice: Archaeologists have found evidence for the animal sacrifice of Canaanite for about 5,000 years ago. Researchers have also discovered that donkeys, sheep, and goats were brought along the Nile River in Egypt to the land of Canaan as sacrificing animals.

Chinese animal sacrifice: Archaeologists have found horses sacrificed in a heap near the tomb of King Duke Jing of Qi, who ruled from 547 to 490 AD in ancient China. Horses' sacrifice has been widespread in China.

On September 28, 2005, China celebrated the 2556th birthday of Confucius, a Chinese philosopher and scholar who lived from 551 to 479 AD and worshipped him. Chinese people wore traditional attire for this cultural celebration, and they offered goat, cow, and pig heads as sacrifices to their gods at the Confucius temples.

African animal sacrifice: In ancient times, even the African people made the largest sacrifices. Animal sacrifices are still made to the gods by the Aboriginal people. Is there any mystery here if the great majority of individuals on the planet carry out the same action? It is true that millions of people have sacrificed animals for centuries in an effort to atone for their sins.

Taoism animal sacrifice: Taiwanese who follow the Taoism religion gather at the temple in Zanzia. On February 23, 2007, each pig weighing up to 900kg was sacrificed to their god. A total of ten pigs, the largest weighing up to 890 kilograms (1,963 pounds), were sacrificed in the annual traditional ritual. The pigs were killed, dressed then spread to make them appear much larger then real size.

***

Why Animal Sacrifices Are Not Now Significant?

Why have many religions lost interest in it today after sacrificing billions of animals in the past? For thousands of years, billions of people have sacrificed billions of animals; was it all for nothing? They offered sacrifices for themselves when they were unable to bear the revenge of Dead-Karma of conscience. They did this only to eradicate dead-karma. Egyptians, Greeks, Mesopotamians, and Romans stopped the sacrifices about a thousand years ago because the benefits of animal sacrifice were so limited and temporary. In India, this has just been realized. Animal sacrifices have been stopped in Hindu temples by the recent legal system. Why do people who once said animal sacrifices were important now stop or minimize them? People offered sacrifices for thousands of years; but why do they now say that animal sacrifices are not needed? No one can say that sacrifice is of no use. If said, it means that we are blaming our ancestor's ritual systems. The people who talk about ancient wisdom, why do they shut their mouths on animal sacrifices? The truth is, people now realized that "the benefits of these sacrifices are minimal and only temporary." This is the reality of the world!

Why are the benefits of animal sacrifices so minimal and temporary? The Pentateuch of the Israelites gives a clear answer for this. As per the Pentateuch, the sacrifices were made only for temporary relief from dead-karma and not for permanent settlement. Look at what happened when the animals were sacrificed:

Leviticus 17:11 For the life of the flesh is in the blood: and I have given it to you upon the altar to make an atonement for your souls: for it is the blood that maketh an atonement for the soul.

The Hebrew word for "atonement" in Leviticus 17:11 is "kaphar." This means covering. Atonement means covering sin. Sin must be covered through atonement. For example, if someone spills the tea on the floor, for urgency, they will cover it with a blanket so that no one can see it. When someone gets home, they are unaware of the tea stain. However, the tea stain is still present and unaltered within the blanket. The animal sacrifices are also the same like covering the stain of the sin. In ancient days, when animal sacrifices were made, the voice of the blood of the sacrificed animals covered the revenging voice of the evil-Dead-Karma (sin). Thus, humans continued to cover their sins with the blood of animals every year. Because sin is hidden, covering granted a temporary release. But within a short period, eventually, the covering voice of the sacrificed animal's blood was overpowered by the dreadful, rising voice of the hidden evil-Dead-Karma. Therefore, the sinful conscience continued to assert them even after sacrifices were made. So they had to pay sacrifices every year for their same dead-karma (same sin).

Hebrews 10:1-4 For the law having a shadow of good things to come, and not the very image of the things, can never with those sacrifices which they offered year by year continually make the comers thereunto perfect. For then would they not have ceased to be offered? because that the worshippers once purged should have had no more conscience of sins. But in those sacrifices there is a remembrance again made of sins every year. For it is not possible that the blood of bulls and of goats should take away sins.

Sacrifices that hide the evil-Dead-Karma (sin) in conscience are never perfect remedy. Animal sacrifices were offered temporarily to receive mercy from God. The sacrifices of the Israelites which had not washed away their sinful conscience were not perfect sacrifices. "Sacrifices that do not wash the conscience from the evil-dead-works are useless sacrifices" God was not pleased with such sacrifices.

Isaiah 1:11 To what purpose is the multitude of your sacrifices unto me? saith the LORD: I am full of the burnt offerings of rams, and the fat of fed beasts; and I delight not in the blood of bullocks, or of lambs, or of he goats.

True sacrifice should not cover sin but must wash away sin completely. Even though the animals are sacrificed in this world, the brutality of evil-Dead-Karma (sin) is unbearable.

Conclusion: Why did the sacrifice of animals fail to remove evil Dead-Works? The sacrifices of animals are not able to wash evil Dead-Works from conscience. If it can do so, people would still insist on sacrificing animals in all religions; is not it? All major religions say, "All should suffer the deadly effects of the Dead-Works". Do you know why the evil Dead-Karma does not perish? There is still a guilty conscience even after the animal sacrifice was made. So the evil Dead-Karma does not perish. The horror of evil Dead-Karma (sin) is unbearable. Even though a sinner offers a sacrifice, the nagging of old guilt in the conscience repeatedly reminds him that his evil Dead-Work (sin) is still in him.

Alms Lost Their Power

(Even after giving alms to the poor and needy, there is evil Dead-Karma's horror in the sinful conscience)

Can money be given in payment for a person's sin? Can charity cleanse the consciousness of the evil Dead-Karma (sin)? In this world, a man may have saved a thousand lives. But would any court in the world spare him if he merely killed one person? By capturing a thousand traitors, one guy may have done a lot of good for the country. But, will any country's judiciary forgive him for the one act of treason he has committed? Certainly not! He will be held accountable and must be punished! No matter how many kind actions a guy performs, his evil will follow him. His conscience continues to taunt his transgression. He will face the punishment eventually. It is the effect of dead karma. Whatever he does for charity and offerings, his Evil-Dead-Karma (sin) will follow him. No charity, no sacrifices can wash away the evil-Dead-Karma (sin) from his conscience.

Hebrews 9:9 Which was a figure for the time then present, in which were offered both gifts and sacrifices, that could not make him that did the service perfect, as pertaining to the conscience;

Conclusion: Why did the alms fail to eliminate man's Evil-dead-karma? If you donate to charity, you will get equal benefits. But he must suffer the punishment for his sin (Evil-dead-karma). All great religions say that one must suffer the evil-Dead Work. Even though a sinner does charity, the nagging old guilty conscience of man is repeatedly reminding him of his Evil-Dead-Works.

Lawcourt Lost Its Power

(Even after receiving punishment in the prison for sin, the horrorful evil Dead-Karma stubbornly glued in the sinful conscience)

"We are not punished for what we've done, but we are punished by our deeds," some say. A thief or murderer is criminalised in court, sentenced in jail, and then released after several years of imprisonment. Do you believe his quilty conscience will depart him? Absolutely not! His guilt will torment him for the rest of his life because of his evil deeds. Why does it torment? This is due to his conscience's storage of "Dead-Karma." That Dead-Karma continues to nag him and remind him of his wrongdoing. The court and prison authorities know how to punish the accused for their crimes, but they do not understand how to eliminate the dreadful Dead-Karma that exists in the conscience of the guilty. No amount of imprisonment can stop the horrors of the Dead-Karma (sin). Do you think that if a guy is sentenced to death and executed, his guilty conscience will depart him when he dies? Not at all! Even after death, the guilty conscience will chase him relentlessly. This is because the Dead-Karma is imprinted in the conscience. No wisdom was able to free man from the dreadful Dead-Karma. The cemented evil Dead-Karma in man's consciousness will get its vengeance without fail.

Conclusion: Why did worldly punishments fail to erase man's Dead-Karma? Even after enduring all punishments, guilty conscience is cemented in man. As a result, Dead-Karma is not erased from man's conscience. All major religions teach that one must endure dead-karma. Even though a wicked person has been imprisoned for a long time, the nagging, old guilt of man's conscience constantly tells him that his Dead-Karma is still cemented in him.

Forgiveness Lost Its Power

(Even after forgiving a man for his sin, the evil Dead-Karma's horror is present in the sinful conscience)

"Forgiving does not erase the bitter past. A healed memory is not a deleted memory. Instead, forgiving what we cannot forget creates a new way to remember." — Louis B. Smedes, Professor of theology and Ethics

What will happen if god forgives a person?: Forgiveness is divine, intelligent, peaceful, admired, and able to heal humans and the world. Yet forgiveness does not have the potential to eliminate the guilt. It can lift its head at any time to avenge the criminal with its own horrorful procedures. When a sin is forgiven, it is covered (hidden), and no man can destroy it. Even if the wife forgives her husband, she can reveal his guilt at any time. When it is forgiven, forgiveness does not completely delete the guilt. Forgiveness does not change the old deeds. This is the nature of every human being. No one can change the common nature of human beings. All major religions say that nature reveals the divine nature of God. The common nature of creatures is the nature of God. So, it is natural that even if God forgives, sin will remain hidden in the court of conscience of sinners. This hidden sin (Dead-Karma) is very dangerous. So, as per religions, God forgives the sinners but sin is not removed, it is hidden in conscience. Sin is terrible. Its vengeance is unending.

What God's forgiveness cannot do?: A study on forgiveness was undertaken at the University of California, Berkeley. Do you understand what forgiveness is, according to the findings of this study? Experts who research or teach forgiveness make it clear that when you forgive, you do not minimise or dismiss the gravity of an offence committed against you. Forgiveness does not imply forgetting or accepting or excusing wrongdoing. Though forgiveness might aid in the mending of a broken relationship, it does not oblige you to reconcile with the person who wronged you or absolve them of legal responsibility.

No one can forgive someone from the depths of their hearts. Even those who forgive are subject to a court of conscience. Wherever the crimes are booked, the same court must investigate the cases, and no other court can try them. How can the Forgiver's court investigate the victim's crimes? As a result, the forgiveness does not come from the depths of the heart.

When you forgive someone, the guilty are momentarily released. The actual harmony of forgiver and sinner, however, suffers. So the harmony of forgiver and sinner continues with caution. When you forgive someone, it does not imply that you must entirely trust him. Even after forgiveness, the brand names of thieves, liars, adulterers, murders, and cheaters remain. When sinners repent and accept forgiveness, their misdeeds are concealed within, but not entirely erased so that they cannot be remembered. Forgiveness is the same as extinguishing a Dead-Karma fire. However, the harshness of flammable substances remains in Dead-Karma. The forgiver lacks the authority and power to remove the flammable element in Dead-Karma. The forgiver does not have the power and authority to remove the combustible substance in Dead-Karma. It can get ignited again at any time to take revenge. The power and authority of Dead-Karma rests on the judiciary of the conscience.

Forgiveness is the same as masking the foul smell. When foul smell is masked, it is not eradicated. It is always possible to reopen it. Once opened, the foul smell will throw back to exercise its judgement. Forgiveness does not have the power, qualification, or authority to remove sin from the sinner. It rests on the authority of the judiciary of the conscience. Who put such guilty feelings in the court of your conscience? Even after when someone forgives you, why does your conscience hurt you? How did you get such a conscience which hurts you without ceasing? Even if God forgives, forgiveness does not completely delete man's sin. This is why Psamist wrote about covering of sin in Psalm 85:2.

Psalms 85:2 Thou hast forgiven the iniquity of thy people, thou hast covered all their sin. Selah.

Even though God forgives, sin is just covered, not removed. The state of the sinner's conscience will remain unchanged. Yet, he is guilty in his own court.

Conclusion: Even if God forgives man's sin, man will still have Dead-Karma in his self-court called conscience. Therefore, all religions say that each person should reap the reward for their deeds.

Punishments Lost Their Power

(Even after receiving punishment in the hell for sin, there is evil Dead-Karma's horror in the sinful conscience)

O Death, where is your sting? O Hades, where is your victory? – 1 Corinthians 15:55

There is no one in this world who is sinless. We are all sinners. So everyone must be condemned on earth, and everyone must live on to suffer in hell. Do you believe that if a guy is sentenced to death and executed, his guilty conscience will depart him when he dies? Not at all! The guilty conscience will plague him till he dies. Even if a guy is punished in hell, his guilty conscience would kill him again and again, right? Dead-Karma is always hungry to take revenge. Man would have done many good things in his life, yet even a minor error would render him wicked, and his conscience would be hostile to him.

James 2:10 For whosoever shall keep the whole law, and yet offend in one *point,* he is guilty of all.

Many people underestimate the consequences of sin. They dig their own grave by claiming that this is not sin. It is extremely hazardous. They will be opposed by their conscience. Will the sinner be welcomed to paradise after experiencing the torments of hell? Absolutely not! Whatever the penalty is given in the hell too, the Evil-Dead-Karma is still at work in their conscience. Who will deliver you from the terrors of conscience? Who can liberate man from the conscience that underscores the Dead-Karma (sin)? How may individuals with a contaminated conscience approach God? Isn't the conscience prick you when you go to your wife, children, and parents after seeing nude pictures on computer or mobile phones? Does not the same conscience prick you when you stand in front of God? Is not the sinful conscience alienating man from standing before God? Sin is a terrible stain on the human conscience. The sinful stains in conscience are dangerously overwhelming.

Adam's luminous spirit body left him when he sinned. He died in the luminous Spirit's body. Adam's transgression was promptly punished. Even if he was quickly punished, could he confront God as he usually did? He couldn't do it. He hid himself from the presence of God. Even though Adam was punished for his Dead-Karma (sin), the Dead-Karma (sin) was strongly glued in his conscience. Similarly, even if man is punished in hell for his sin, his guilty conscience will remain unchanged. It will keep on taking revenge. This is why the soul that goes to hell will continue to be punished for its sin. There will be no end to it. As per Hinduism, for the crime of single lie on earth, the tongue of a sinner will be cut repeatedly in the hell without ceasing and the tongue of sinner also keep growing to be punished without ceasing. The Garuda Purana of Hinduism says that there is no end to this. Almost all religions say that there is endless punishment in hell. The soul is indestructible by humans. Only God can destroy it. This continues until the soul, along with its conscience, is finally destroyed.

Conclusion: The punishments of hell failed because man's Dead-Karma could not be erased from the conscience. Dead-Karma certainly not deleted even if sinner is suffered in hell. All great religions say that man must endure Dead-Karma endlessly. Even though a sinner is punished by hell for the crime he committed, the nagging of old guilty conscience repeatedly reminds his sins.

The Disturbing Story Of Conscience

The person that loses their conscience has nothing left worth keeping. – *Izaak Walton*

Conscience is the invisible force that shapes the world. It is both guide and judge, a witness to both wrong and right.

- It creates the laws that govern individuals, societies, institutes, and nations.
- It guards the spirit, the soul, and the mind.
- It calls us toward mercy, love, and care for the needy.
- It is the silent power that holds the world together.

Without conscience, everything collapses. No other court is as just as the court of conscience. When a man lives by good conscience, he is the happiest of all—peace rules his heart.

The gift of conscience is the source of wisdom, a light that shines on both rich and poor, educated and uneducated, king and servant alike. When the voice of conscience is honored, society flourishes.

But when that voice is silenced, destruction follows. Ignored conscience does not die—it returns as something darker: Dead-Karma.

- Every crime, every betrayal, every act of cruelty awakens conscience. And when guilt refuses to die, it hardens into Dead-Karma.

- Dead-Karma is the avenger of conscience.
- Dead-Karma follows the wrongdoer like a dark shadow.
- It cannot be silenced by rituals, sacrifices, forgiveness, wealth, law, or power. No bribe can buy it, no excuse can hide it, no punishment can erase it. Dead-Karma remains.
- He could no longer remain a silent servant of a broken system. His conscience drove him beyond the law, transforming him into something new—an avenger of injustice.

Vengeance brought no peace. Dead-Karma grew heavier with every step. Justice through revenge only multiplies guilt. No human strategy or power has succeeded in destroying the kingdom of Dead-Karma (the sin). Mankind is struck in the darkness of Dead-Karma (the sin).

❖

THE GEOMETRY OF RUIN

If you do not slay sin (Dead-Karma),

sin (Dead-Karma) will slay you

- Charles Spurgeon

We've seen in the last passages that Dead-Karma is nothing but dead-works; and evil-dead-works are sins. I could have written the word "sin" directly. But reason for mentioning "Dead-Karma or dead-work" is that, It is possible to provide a clearer and better explanation of the term Dead-Karma or dead-work than the word sin. That is why I continue to use this word. The wages of sin is death. That is, the wages of sin is destruction. It can also be said that the wages of Dead-Karma is destruction. In summary, let us examine how dead-karma emerged and began to DISENGINEER human beings piece by piece.

1) The first man shattered the likeness of God within him.
2) Shattering of likeness of God was connected to the fruit of the tree of knowing good and evil.
3) This fruit gave man the knowledge of good and evil

4) The knowledge of good and evil is nothing but conscience.
5) The conscience gave the law to men & also stored evil-Dead-Karma in it.
6) The most important seals were removed from man by the rule of Dead-Karma. This means that man is disengineered piece by piece.
7) Man began to perish.
8) Dead-Karma (sin) became the cause of all the misery of man.

We will go into depth on how man is heading toward destruction (becoming disengineered) after a couple of his primary seals were damaged.

Earnest Of The Spirit: The First Portion Of Man Was Disengineered

<u>The seal of the "Earnest of the Spirit" was given:</u> Adam was sealed with the Spirit of God. This seal was a wonderful seal. This was the seal which symbolized that man belongs to God. This seal of the Holy Spirit was the hub holding all the spiritual accessories, gifts, and also other perfect divine seals.

<u>After sinning, the seal of the "Earnest of the Spirit" was removed:</u> As soon as man fell into sin, the horror and terror of Dead-Karma judged man. The earnest seal of the Spirit was cut off from men. thus, the hub of spiritual accessories, gifts, and also other perfect divine seals was missing in man.

Seed Of God: The Second Portion Of Man Was Disengineered

The earnest seal of the Spirit was given as the seed of God: the life that arises from the seed imitates the seed perfectly. Adam was created in the Spirit of God. That Spirit was God's seed. So he walked in as per the likeness of God (Seed of God). When a man is born of the flesh, the seed of the flesh enters him. As a result, fleshly appetites, lust, pride, and pleasures begin to lead man. God implanted his seed in Adam on the day he was created. This seed is nothing more than God's Spirit. thus, spiritual genetics existed in man.

John 3:6 That which is born of the flesh is flesh; and that which is born of the Spirit is spirit.

The seed of God was withdrawn from Adam once he sinned: As soon as Adam fell into sin, he lost the seal of the Spirit. How can a man be a father to a child if his seed is not present? Cannot! Adam lost his status as God's Son when the seed of God left him. Adam became the flesh's descendants when he became a man of the flesh and acted in accordance with the flesh.

Romans 9:8 That is, they which are the children of the flesh, these are not the children of God: but the children of the promise are counted for the seed.

As the seed of God's Spirit drifted away Adam, so did spiritual genetics. Following the fall, Adam imitated according to his flesh. As a result, it was established that Adam was born in fleshy genetics at the moment of his sin.

Son Of God Status: The Third Portion Of Man Was Disengineered

Son of God status was given: The spirit of God was in Adam. The first man was led by the Spirit of God because the Spirit of God was in him as a seed. Scripture also says that whoever is led by the Spirit of God, they are the son of God (Romans 8:14). Adam was called the son of God because the spirit of God was leading Adam as a seed.

Adam's Son of God status was taken away after sin: When Adam sinned, he lost the seed of God; Adam lost the privilege to call himself as son of God.

The Qualification To The Kingdom Of God: The Fourth Portion Of Man Was Disengineered

The qualification to join the Kingdom of God was given: The seal of God's Spirit was inside Adam. Adam was guided by the Holy Spirit in this way. God's kingdom remained in him until God's Spirit remained in Adam as a seal. Adam was enjoying God's wonderful realm. God's kingdom is nothing more than the work of the Holy Spirit.

Matthew 12:28 But if I cast out devils by the Spirit of God, then the kingdom of God is come unto you.

After sin, the qualification to join the Kingdom of God was removed: When Adam sinned, the Holy Spirit left Adam. Because the Holy Spirit went far away from him, Adam was turned away from God and also from God's kingdom.

The Barrier That Prohibited Condemnation: The Fifth Portion Of Man Was Disengineered

The Spirit barrier was given to forbid condemnation: Only those who walk in the Spirit have no judgment. The day Adam was created, the Spirit of God was given to Adam as a barrier to forbid the condemnation for his sin. Only those who walk in the flesh have laws and condemnation and for them, there is no barrier to forbid the condemnation.

Galatians 5:18 But if ye be led of the Spirit, ye are not under the law.

Before sin, the Spirit of God was a seal of earnest in Adam. Until he was led by the Spirit of God, he was not under any judgment. So he had no condemnation by any law.

Romans 8:1 There is therefore now no condemnation to them which are in Christ Jesus, who walk not after the flesh, but after the Spirit.

After sin, the Spirit barrier to forbid condemnation was removed: After sin, because the Spirit of God was withdrawn from Adam, he had become a fleshly man and had been judged by his walk of the flesh. His descendants also suffered a terrible judgment.

The Seven Spirits: The Sixth Portion Of Man Was Disengineered

Seven Spirits were given to Adam: The prophet Isaiah saw in his vision that the Spirit of the Lord rested upon Jesus Christ. These Spirits were seven. The seven spirits of Jesus Christ are part of the likeness and image of God.

Isaiah 11:2 And the spirit of the LORD shall rest upon him, the spirit of wisdom and understanding, the spirit of counsel and might, the spirit of knowledge and of the fear of the LORD;

Do you know what these spirits are?

1. The Spirit of the LORD 2. The spirit of wisdom

3. The spirit of understanding 4. The spirit of counsel

5. The spirit of might, 6. The spirit of knowledge 7. The spirit of the fear of the LORD

Similar to God's likeness and image, the first man had seven spirits. Let's see how the first man received the seal of these seven spirits that the Messiah had received.

- The Spirit of the Lord: The Spirit of the Lord descended upon Adam. The Spirit of the Lord who descended upon Samson would have descended upon Adam before he sinned.

  Judges 15:14 And when he came unto Lehi, the Philistines shouted against him: and the Spirit of the LORD came mightily upon him, and the cords that were upon his arms became as flax that was burnt with fire, and his bands loosed from off his hands.

- Spirit of Wisdom: Giving wisdom is one of the works of the Spirit of God. God gives the spirit of wisdom only when the fear of the Lord comes in a person.

Ephesians 1:17 That God of our Lord Jesus Christ, the Father of glory, may give unto you the spirit of wisdom and revelation in the knowledge of him:

The day Adam was created; he was filled with the Spirit of the wisdom of God because the fear of the Lord and the spirit of God were upon him.

- Spirit of understanding: Since the Holy Spirit was with Adam, the spirit of understanding was within Adam. So Adam was an understanding man.

1Corinthians 12:8 For to one is given by the Spirit the word of wisdom; to another the word of knowledge by the same Spirit;

Psalms 119:130 The entrance of thy words giveth light; it giveth understanding unto the simple.

- Spirit of Counsel: The Holy Spirit gave counsel to Adam because he had the seal of the Holy Spirit. Adam walked in the direction of God since he was created.
- Spirit of might: Adam was strong because he was filled with the spirit of the might. He had no weakness.

Acts 1:8 But ye shall receive power, after that the Holy Ghost is come upon you: and ye shall be witnesses unto me both in Jerusalem, and in all Judaea, and in Samaria, and unto the uttermost part of the earth.

- Spirit of knowledge: The Spirit of God gives universal knowledge. The Spirit enlightens mankind through words, through vision, through prophecy and through dreams. When Adam had received the Spirit of God, before sin, he was given the knowledge of heaven and earth through the Spirit of God. Adam knew what is going to happen. For Adam, everything was bright, his future was not dark. The spirit of the knowledge of God was within him.

Spirit of the fear of the LORD: It is good to fear the Lord. The fear of the Lord is the beginning of wisdom (Judges 1: 7). But the fear of man will bring snare. We read in the Scriptures that whosoever puts his trust in the LORD shall be safe (Judges 29:25). Without God's approval, not everyone can be godly. The spirit of the fear of the Lord rested upon Adam when he was created.

After sin, seven Spirits of God Removed from man. But seven spirits of evil encamped in man: Before Adam sinned, we saw that Adam had seven spirits in him. This was the likeness and image of God. But after the sin, the seven spirits of God left Adam. Because the Holy Spirit performs seven kinds of work, the seven types of works are named after the seven. Adam lost all seven spirits of light as the Holy Spirit left him.

The unclean spirits encamped in man after the Holy Spirit was removed.

> *Matthews 12:43-45 When the unclean spirit is gone out of a man, he walketh through dry places, seeking rest, and findeth none. Then he saith, I will return into my house from whence I came out; and when he is come, he findeth it empty, swept, and garnished. Then goeth he, and taketh with himself seven other spirits more wicked than himself, and they enter in and dwell there: and the last state of that man is worse than the first. Even so shall it be also unto this wicked generation.*

Unclean spirits that are in fallen man:

1) The Spirit of Slavery (Romans 8:15)

2) The Spirit of Weakness (Luke 13: 11-13)

3) The Spirit of Slumber (Romans 11: 8)

4) The Spirit of Fear (II Timothy 1: 7)

5) The seducing spirit (I John 4: 6, I Timothy 4: 1)

6) The Spirit of jealousy (Numbers 5:14)

7) The lying Spirit (II Chronicles 18: 20-22)

Fruits Of The Spirit: The Seventh Portion Of Man Was Disengineered

The nine fruits of man were given to man as God's seal: The nine fruits of Spirit are listed below.

1) God is love (1 John 4: 8),

2) God is joyful (Zephaniah 3:17),

3) God is God of peace (Romans 15:33)

4) God is long-suffering (1 Peter Psalm 86:15)

5) Gentleness of God is great of God (2 Samuel 22:36)

6) God is Goodness God (Luke 18:19)

7) God is faithful within Him

8) The meekness of God is mentioned in Bible (2 Corinthians 10: 1)

9) God is in control within Himself. There is no violation of each other within the trinity. These are the fruits of God.

Adam was fulfilled with the Holy Spirit. So Adam was spiritual. The Holy Spirit does not ordinarily exist within a human being. But as soon as the Spirit comes into a man, the fruits of the Spirit begin to appear in him. The Holy Spirit is the one who recognizes sin and leads man in the holy way. Spiritually holy fruit must have been found in Adam before sin.

Galatians 5:22-23 But the fruit of the Spirit is love, joy, peace, longsuffering, gentleness, goodness, faith, Meekness, temperance: against such there is no law.

The nine fruits of God are the likeness of God. Because the Spirit of God was perfect in Adam, he also received the fruit of God on the day he was created.

After sin, the nine fruits were removed: The fruit of the Spirit was found in Adam as long as the Holy Spirit was in him.

Galatians 5:22-23 But the fruit of the Spirit is love, joy, peace, longsuffering, gentleness, goodness, faith, Meekness, temperance: against such there is no law.

The Holy Spirit does not dwell in an unclean temple. Scripture says that the body of man is the temple of God. The temple of God is holy.

1Co 3:16-17 Know ye not that ye are the temple of God, and that the Spirit of God dwelleth in you? If any man defile the temple of God, him shall God destroy; for the temple of God is holy, which temple ye are.

Because the Holy Spirit departed Adam after he sinned, he had lost the fruits of the Spirit. The flesh dominated him due to a lack of the Holy Spirit. As a result, Adam received the unclean fruit of the flesh. After Adam fell into sin, the wicked fruit of the flesh was discovered in him. The unclean products of the flesh are as follows:

Galatians 5:19-21 Now the works of the flesh are manifest, which are these; Adultery, fornication, uncleanness, lasciviousness, Idolatry, witchcraft, hatred, variance, emulations, wrath, strife, seditions, heresies, Envyings, murders, drunkenness, revellings, and such like: of the which I tell you before, as I have also told you in time past, that they which do such things shall not inherit the kingdom of God.

Holiness: The Eight Portion Of Man Was Disengineered

<u>The seal of God's nature in man:</u> Is God-like nature a seal of God? Yes. Behavior can be described as the nature of God.

2Peter 1:4 Whereby are given unto us exceeding great and precious promises: that by these ye might be partakers of the divine nature, having escaped the corruption that is in the world through lust

In the above verse, the Apostle Peter wrote about the divine nature. He had mentioned a Greek word "Theos phusis" (like φύσις -theios phusis) for divine nature. The meaning of this word is "God-like growth by germination". This also means, "Budding and growing in the likeness of God". Everything that acts like God is the likeness of God. Practices such as obedience, being holy, being righteous, and loving are all natures of man.

Ephesians 4:24 And that ye put on the new man, which after God is created in righteousness and true holiness.

If we act like God in righteousness and holiness, it is the nature of God. God created man in his likeness. Adam also possessed such a likeness of God.

God is holy. Holiness is the likeness of God. On the day that God created Adam, God created Adam Holy like Him.

After sin, Holiness - the likeness of God was removed in man: There was sin was in Adam when he walked in the flesh. The seal of holiness had left Adam, and the impure seal of sin had infected Adam.

Righteousness: The Ninth Portion Of Man Was Disengineered

Righteousness - the likeness of God was impressed in man: God is righteous. It is the likeness of God. On the day that God created Adam, God created Adam in the likeness of righteous of Him.

Ephesians 4:24 And that ye put on the new man, which after God is created in righteousness and true holiness.

The fleshly mind is unclean. Before sinning, Adam walked in the Spirit of God, not in the flesh. So Adam was not a sinner. Adam grew up in the likeness of God's righteousness. He had the likeness of righteousness as God did.

After sin, righteousness - the likeness of God was removed in man: After sinning, Adam lost his holiness and became unclean and lost his righteousness; became unrighteous. His offspring were born in the same likeness. This is because the spirit of God in which Adam walked, left him. The seal of the righteousness of God was removed from Adam.

Physical Body: The Tenth Portion Of Man Was Disengineered (Second Death)

Do you know what physical death means in the eyes of this world?

The death of the physical body is nothing but the separation of the soul from the physical body. After the corpse is separated, the corpse becomes soil. Only the soul of man stands alone as a real man. The death of physical body happens to all who are born of Adam. Even if a man dies in the flesh, the real human soul is still alive. This was the second death for Adam. What is death? Death is nothing but the separation of one body from another body. Death is dismantling one body from another body. In the second death, the soul travels naked to its destinated place which is away from the fleshy world. The scripture says that the wages of sin (Dead-Karma) is death.

Body Of Light: The Eleventh Portion Of Man Was Disengineered (First Death)

Poet is *someone who* never *forgets they* were *born* naked - Martin Rubin

Can be shy, but I'm not shy with my body. Everyone is naked under their clothes - so what? Cameron Richardson

Do you know, what is big confusion for many people? God commanded that you will die on the day you eat the fruit of the tree of knowing good and evil. When Adam ate the apple, did he die the same day? If Adam died on the same day, one could wonder why he was still living. Some claim that Adam's soul passed away. Real man is Adam's Soul. Adam could not have existed at all if the soul had died. Some claim he died in the Spirit. The spirit connects the soul and body like a silver cord, as we discovered in earlier chapters. His flesh and soul would have been torn apart if he had died in the Spirit, and his physical body would have separated from the soul and died. Others claim that

God foretold Adam's death in the future. But God did not foretell what would happen in the future; God specified that on the same day Adam will die. If Adam did not die on the same day, why did God not fulfill this command: "On the day of eating the fruit Adam will die"? Why didn't Adam and Eve die that day? Questions arise as to whether God has lied? Even though many theologians have offered a variety of explanations, those explanations are not convincible to the mind. Finally, only the image and likeness of God give us the most accurate and clear explanation for this. Adam died as God had commanded on the day of eating the fruit of the tree of the knowing good and evil. If you comprehend Adam's second death, you can discover how Adam's first death happened. This will help you realise how Adam's first death happened. The separation of a person's physical body from his or her soul marks the second death. Similarly, the first death occurred when the glorious body of light (another layer of body interwoven in Adam) departed man. Let's explore how the first man was interwoven with the glorious body of light. Moreover, we are going to explore how the first death occurred to Adam and Eve.

Adam had a glorious body of light before he sinned. There are many of proofs for this. God is glorious. Man is created in the likeness and image of God. Whether or if Adam had a glorious body of light similar to God's is the key question. If this question can be answered, not only will the mystery surrounding Adam's first death be resolved, but also a great number of other mysteries. We'll examine the facts to see if Adam had a glorious body of light or not.

The evidences for the existed glorious body of light

Moses is a witness to the fact that the first man was clothed with the glorious body of light: Adam was walking with the LORD God who was a consuming fire (Deuteronomy 4:24). God also appeared as a light. Many people wonder how man could have appeared like a light. Moses' face shined while he was with God on Mount Sinai. The people were frightened to approach Moses. Moses covered his face to conceal his brightness.

Exodus 34:29-30 And it came to pass, when Moses came down from mount Sinai with the two tables of testimony in Moses' hand, when he came down from the mount, that Moses wist not that the skin of his face shone while he talked with him. And when Aaron and all the children of Israel saw Moses, behold, the skin of his face shone; and they were afraid to come nigh him.

Imagine how Moses, who had only been with God for forty days, shined so brightly. Adam could see and hear God walking, and God could stand in front of him. God was with Adam from the beginning, when he was fashioned by God's own hands and breathed God's breath into him. God also watched Adam's transformation into a living soul. The first man talked to God face to face, God trained him, and the first man named every animal that God brought him. The LORD God created Eve from the rib He took from Adam, and He brought her to Adam. God was so close to Adam for such a long period more than Moses. Imagine how Adam must have shined so brightly when he was so near to the LORD God, who was a blazing fire! Consider how the first man, Adam, who was closer to God than Moses, must have shined brightly before he fell into sin! Before sinning, Adam had the appearance of a light, and he was clothed in the body of glorious light. The nakedness of Adam's physical body was clothed by a garment of glorious light, just as the human physical body now covers the nakedness of the soul.

1. *The first man was clothed with the glorious body of light and stood among those who were clothed in glorious light:* Many ethnic tribes continue to live naked even today. If they're all naked

in the crowd, no naked man would be ashamed to go naked in that crowd. There is no need for a naked woman to hide herself in a naked gathering because everyone is naked. But, when everyone is covering their nakedness, does a man not hurry away and cover his nakedness? Adam, who was created in the likeness of God, appeared with a body of light. But Adam became naked after sinning because his garment of glory was taken from him. So Adam covered himself from being naked in front of God. Adam was unable to stand before God, who was dressed in glory (Psalm 104:1).

Genesis 3:8 And they heard the voice of the LORD God walking in the garden in the cool of the day: and Adam and his wife hid themselves from the presence of the LORD God amongst the trees of the garden.

Adam was left without his garment of glory, so he stood naked. Today, all humans are naked under their own clothes. They therefore make every effort to conceal their nakedness.

2Corinthians 5:2-3 For in this we groan, earnestly desiring to be clothed upon with our house which is from heaven: If so be that being clothed we shall not be found naked.

2. *God covers Himself with light as a garment; So Adam too was covered himself with the light as a garment: Bible clearly tells us that God covers Himself with light as a garment*

Psalms 104:2 Who coverest thyself with light as with a garment: who stretchest out the heavens like a curtain:

We read in the Scriptures that men who conquer will be clothed in white garments (Revelation 3: 5). We also read in Revelation 3:18 that qualified people should be clothed with the white garment of light so that there is no nakedness seen in them.

We should not think of this garment as ordinary. Do not think that a weaver has woven this white garment with threads or earthly polymers. There are no weavers with God or God does not weave like men do. This white garment which is mentioned in the scripture is called in Greek leukos (Λευκός). The word comes from the Greek word Luke (λύκη-lukē). It means "light". You can also see this word in the "Strong" dictionary. If so, those who walk with Jesus Christ in the immortal body and also those who are conquered to be in the eternity will not be clothed in a garment of woven by threads or earthly polymers, but in the garment of glorious light. This is an illuminating body. Adam was clothed in with such a illuminating body.

Revelation 7:13 And one of the elders answered, saying unto me, What are these which are arrayed in white robes? and whence came they?

Arrayed (Arrayed: περιβάλλω (periballō) means that *threw* all *around*)

The saints found in heaven were dressed in white. We read in Greek, the original language in which this scripture was written, that these white-clad men were not ordinary, but were capable of blowing radiation around them. The word "periballō" (περιβάλλω- periballō) has been used in the Greek language for blowing light rays. It is correctly translated into the English Scriptures. The scripture says that such a ray of light should be restored in man. The garment to be worn indicates the light-blowing body of a man. This need to be redeemed which was lost in Adam and his descendants. Only this garment will cover the nakedness of human being permanent.

2Corinthians 5:2-3 For in this we groan, earnestly desiring to be clothed upon with our house which is from heaven: If so be that being clothed we shall not be found naked.

Adam lost his glorious body when he sinned. As the garment of light had passed away from him, he realized that he was naked.

3. *The likeness of God is a witness to the fact that Adam had a glorious body of light: According to the prophet Ezekiel, God was encircled by a rainbow of light. According to the same prophet, this brightness of God was the likeness of the glory of God.*

Ezekiel 1:28 As the appearance of the bow that is in the cloud in the day of rain, so was the appearance of the brightness round about. This was the appearance of the likeness of the glory of the LORD. And when I saw it, I fell upon my face, and I heard a voice of one that spake.

Note the word "likeness". Scripture says that even brightness of God is His likeness. Scripture says that God created man in his Likeness. Therefore, Adam must have been clothed in garment of light, to be in the likeness of the God. If man were to be in the likeness according to God, many would wonder what would be the difference between man and God.

Prior to mass production, a rocket engineer will programme and shape rockets in accordance with the appearance and shape of the model rocket. The likeness and shape of the production rockets are the same as the model rockets, despite the fact that the energy level, size, and internal mysteries of the production rockets may be different from those of the model rocket. Although man is in the likeness of God, all the energies, programs, life sources and guidance that man needs are all from God. Since Adam was created in the likeness and image of God, he was supposed to remain in the likeness and image of God.

4. The spirit and the light are the same in the spiritual realm: The Bible claims that God is both light and spirit (John 4:24, 1 John 1:

5). What does this imply? Is God Light or Spirit? Which of these is true, you might wonder. We've seen in the previous book (God-like Engineering-I) that the Spirit of God appears as light. So God was shining as the light to those who were watching from the outside. God is therefore both light and spirit at the same time. This is truth, not a paradox.

Islam says that God is light; Judaism says that God is light; Christianity says that God is light, and Hindu leaders said that God is light. This is true. Becoming a light blowing person is the image and likeness of God. Man must have been created in the same likeness.

Many people may wonder how God's glory might become God's body. The Bible provides a clear answer to this question. According to the Scriptures, the light is the Holy Spirit. We also learn that God's light is life. According to the Bible, Jesus' life was light (John 1: 4), and the Spirit also brings life (John 6:63, 2 Corinthians 3: 6). The spirit, light, and life are all the same here. If this is the case, the Spirit around God must have been life, and that life must have been God. So light is God's likeness. On the day Adam was created, God imprinted His likeness into him.

5. According to scripture, the body of light will be redeemed in man - This demonstrates that Adam had a body of light: If someone loses something, they will wait for it to be recovered. Returning mortgaged properties, jewellery, or valuables is known as redemption. If someone has been hijacked by an adversary, it is about redeeming them if they are restored. Take a look at the following scriptures as well.

Ephesians 4:30 And grieve not the holy Spirit of God, whereby ye are sealed unto the day of redemption.

Ephesians 1:14 Which is the earnest of our inheritance until the redemption of the purchased possession, unto the praise of his glory.

What is the day of redemption? What to recover? Why to wait with the earnest seal of the Spirit to redemption? This kind of questions usually comes to everyone's mind. What do we still lost? Why do we wait? In the book of Romans, we read that we need to redeem our body. Even those who are now alive in the flesh are deprived of the most important body what was lost. That body is nothing but the glorious body of light.

Romans 8:23 And not only they, but ourselves also, which have the firstfruits of the Spirit, even we ourselves groan within ourselves, waiting for the adoption, to wit, the redemption of our body.

After man has regained the body of this glorious light, this body of light is going to make man shine like the sun.

Matthew 13:43 Then shall the righteous shine forth as the sun in the kingdom of their Father. Who hath ears to hear, let him hear.

Matthew 13:43 Then shall the righteous shine forth as the sun in the kingdom of their Father. Who hath ears to hear, let him hear.

Adam lost the body of such a glorious light. From the day Adam lost the glorious body of light, all his descendants also were also born without the glorious body of light. So, all human beings are born naked. We are waiting for this lost body to be recovered. We are now living within the earthly tent called flesh with groaning (2 Corinthians 5:4). This is not our the glorious body. Since everyone is waiting for the redemption of the glorious body of light, it is true that Adam was in the Garden of Eden with the glorious body of light.

The Body Of Light Has Been Removed

Nakedness of Adam: The first man declared that he was naked after sinning. Was he, nonetheless, naked before sin? That is the question. Adam was not, in fact, naked. He had a glorious light body. Adam was born with the body of the royal glory, which is the royal attire, on the day he was born. Adam's first death exposes Adam's nakedness (we will continue to read more on this in the later passages)

(1) Death of Adam: Even though God had told Adam not to eat the forbidden fruit, Adam ate the fruit. So he died on the same day.

Genesis 2:17 But of the tree of the knowledge of good and evil, thou shalt not eat of it: for in the day that thou eatest thereof thou shalt surely die.

We will go into detail about the mysteries that abound in this spiritual death. We've learned in the preceding chapter that physical death was the separation of the human body and soul. The first man had three bodies. They are:

i. The soul as a body

ii. The physical body

iii. The body of glorious light (It covered the nakedness of the human flesh. Adam had no sense of nakedness before he sinned because the glorious body of light covered his physical body).

We've seen in the preceding chapter that Adam possessed the body of light. When Adam sinned, the body of light was separated from him. What is death? Now people say, "Death is the separation of the body from the soul." Death is hence the separating of one body from another. Similat to this second death, in the first death of Adam, his body of light was separated from his physical body. This separation of two bodies was the first death of Adam and Eve. So their physical body stood naked. Adam and Eve met their first death.

In the second death, after the death of the physical body, the naked soul will be restless enduring pains. Likewise, in the first death of Adam, the flesh is restless with its nakedness and pains.

2Corinthins 5:2-3 For in this we groan, earnestly desiring to be clothed upon with our house which is from heaven: If so be that being clothed we shall not be found naked.

Every man is born dead: I have a non-Christian cousin brother. One day, he sent me a WhatsApp message describing his experience. The message read like this, "I heard you're going to hell after death, but I have a feeling that we died somewhere else and ended ourselves in this hell on the earth!" This made me think profoundly. This is entirely correct. Adam was in the Garden of Eden, which was similar to Paradise. He died in Eden after the body of light that had covered him was removed. Then the dead Adam was brought to this cursed land. Adam experienced hell on the cursed earth. Every human being born from Adam's children is born into the cursed earth known as hell on Earth. Every individual born on this planet is come dead.

Death is like a hurricane. Death does not stop once. Hurricanes in the sky will continue to accumulate down on the surface of the earth, and it will accumulate in many layers. Such is the death of man.

Man's mortality does not end with his death. It would continue to descend into the bottomless hole for many more layers. In the book "scientific wonders of the Bible," I wrote about the "three wave mystery of every event in the world." Read this book thoroughly; these mysterious waves are both Bible mysteries and world event's mysteries.

There are three waves mysteries for every occurrence in this world, as well as for many key events in the Bible. There are also three waves of death. The first death wave began with Adam's death. The second death is the death of the fleshly body. This is the second death wave. The third death is the death of the soul. It will be terrifying and far worse than the last two deaths. The soul will become entangled in the final hurricane. This is the third wave of death in the life humans.

(2) *The wisdom of babies - Babies cry when they are born to this world:* *Like humans, animals, insects, and also which live in the water are born from the womb of mother. In this, man is the only one who is born with screaming noise. Why the pain of birth is terrible for man? There is pain of birth in the creatures as well! Then, why don't they shout like human babies at birth? If the babies do not cry during birth, why is the practice of tap and make the babies to cry? Why this mystery exists?* In the book of Genesis, the pain of childbirth is a curse for women. However, babies crying are not a curse! But why are they crying?

The Garden of Eden was a paradise which was given to men. After man sinned and died, he was cast out of the Garden of Eden and sent to the cursed land. This earth is the first hell for men, because it was cursed and was subject to the illusion of uncertainty. Every newborn is born with the knowledge that he or she is being born into hell. God has revealed such secrets to the baby that are hidden to the wisemen and educated. Therefore, human babies cry when they are born into this earth to alert mankind to know this mystery.

Matthew 11:25 At that time Jesus answered and said, I thank thee, O Father, Lord of heaven and earth, because thou hast hid these things from the wise and prudent, and hast revealed them unto babes.

It is painful that even the well-educated wise men lack the wisdom which the before its time ends. babies have!

The tragedies of the world: How is the state of man today? Every man on this earth is full of sufferings. Man's life is full of tribulations, punishments, and disturbances.

Job 14:1-2 Man that is born of a woman is of few days, and full of trouble. He cometh forth like a flower, and is cut down: he fleeth also as a shadow, and continueth not.

What are the tragedies in man's life? Poverty, disease, weakness, unemployment, no peace and honesty in employer and employee, Low pay, wars, racism, language problems, water problems, air problems, natural disasters, pestilences, wars, religious terrorism, corruption, murder, robbery, kidnapping, rape, pride, insecurity, fear, impatience etc. We can keep on listing like this. Who is responsible for all these? This is because man has destroyed the divine seal within him, and died loosing the glorious body of the Spirit.

The Soul: The Twelfth **Portion Of Man Was Disengineered** (Third Death)

What about the third and final death?

1. In Adam's first death, the body of light was removed from Adam. The flesh and the soul fused together remained as a man. This was the first death of Adam.

2. The fleshly body is removed from man on the second death. The soul is now alone and naked in the absence of a physical body. It is the second death that all human experience.

3. In the third death, the soul also will die if not qualified for eternity. thus, the third wave of death completes.

The soul is the real man. In two deaths, the soul looses two bodies and the soul is now lonely. And soul turns out to be completely naked. The complete destruction of man is the death of the soul. This is a cruel death! Do you know why this is a cruel death? The first two deaths were just a separation (dismantling) of bodies. But the third death has nothing to do with separation. If the lonely soul dies, the man will be completely cut off. Nothing will be left out.The death of the soul is the deadliest death of all! So the recovery of this soul is very important. No one can ignore this horrorful death. Adam and Eve did not shout at the first death. In the second death, no one struggle badly to save their life. But there will be agony and a loud cry in the third death. The soul must suffer all the pain alone without the body of light and body of flesh. Its pain is so terrible. It is the horrorful death of every human.

In the first death - the man who left the body of light was sent to the earth which was already cursed, tormented, and sweaty.

In the second death - the soul is sent to the hell which is full of agonies.

In the third death, the soul has no place to stay - It is thrown into the bottomless pit. This is a horrible hell where the human soul falls to death. Man is got caught in a hurricane of death! This is horror and horror! There is no limit to the transcendence of Dead-Karma. It DISENGINEERs human being little by little and leaves nothing in him.

Wages Of Sin Is Disengineering

The wages of sin is nakedness. This nakedness is nothing but death. As the body of light was removed from the flesh, the fleshy body became naked. The first death was caused by the first nakedness. The second death was caused by second nakedness. When the fleshy body is removed from the soul in the second death, the soul starts its journey naked. This second nakedness is also the wages of sin. So every time you stand naked, you simply remember the first death of first man in the body of light. No one can deny this fact. When people are publically made naked by force, they feel the seriousness of the punishment and intensity of their embrassement. They feel something they lost. The same kind of feeling Adam had. This is nothing but the removal of cloth of body of light. The dead-karma disengineers man little by little and finally makes him nothing. Seriously mankind need immediate freedom from this horror.

THE FORMULA

If you do not slay sin (Dead-Karma) sin (Dead-Karma) will slay you - Charles Spurgeon

In the previous chapters, we've learned the listed below.

(1) The sacrifices of animals could not wash away the Dead-Karma (sin)

(2) Alms could not wash away the Dead-Karma (sin)

(3) Imprisonment could not wash away the Dead-Karma (sin)

(4) Forgiveness could not wash away the Dead-Karma (sin)

(5) The penalties of hell could not wash away the Dead-Karma (sin)

(6) No other form of worship or ritual in the world could not wash away the Dead-Karma (sin)

According to all great religions, everyone must experience the consequences of Dead-Karma (sin). Horror of Guilty conscience does not get abolished from Dead-Karma after all forms of worship. Where is this Dead-Karma lurking? It sneaks up on the conscience. To eliminate the effects of the Dead-Karma (sin), one must remove the Dead-Karma (sin). Only the removal of Dead-Karma will liberate man completely.

The oil-based cleaner will be able to remove the oil-based stains, while the water-based cleanser is unable to do so. Similar to this, an oil-based cleanser cannot remove water-based stains but a water-based cleaner will remover water based stains. Chemical cleaners are used to remove stains that have a chemical base. Dirt on the clothing can be removed with soap. To clean the toilet of debris, people use acid based. Teeth can also be cleaned with toothpaste. Silver and gold are cleaned using different liquids. The question now is, if each of them has a cleanser, what should be utilised to remove the Dead-Karma that is bonded in the conscience of a man?

People died from pestilences in massive numbers until a medicinal breakthrough. Everyone knew the sickness was on its way. But no one knew how to get rid of pestilence or what the disease was like at the time. Until World War I, more troops perished through sickness than from the sword. Louis Pasteur, a medical scientist, first researched how pandemics or epidemics originate and then devised methods to eliminate them. As a result, he was titled "the Savior of Mankind." He is also recognised as the Father of Immunology and the Founder of Microbiology. He identified the diseases and their characteristics. As a result of his discovery, he was the first to His innovation treated diseases such as anthrax, smallpox, and rabies. He also established the medical science field of bacteriology. As an example, consider a rabid dog bite. It is extremely easy to recognise the nature of disease caused by dog bite if you know the nature of viruses in a dog. Similarly, if we understand the qualities of Dead-Karma (sin) in man, we may quickly locate its destroyer. Religions have struggled for thousands of years to figure out how to destroy the Dead-Karma (sin). First and foremost, we must understand the nature and power of the Dead-Karma (sin). Then we must determine the kind and strength of the substance capable of destroying Dead-Karma (sin). We must discover the core cause of Dead-Karma, as well as its ruins, traits, and strength. It is impossible to deface Dead-Karma without knowing all of these.

The Nature Of Dead-Karma And Its Remover

What exactly makes up Dead-Karma?: Conscience is the voice that is produced in man. The conscience is loud enough to tell a man what is good and what is evil. Dead-Karma (sin) is also a voice that is concentrated in the human conscience. Dead-Karma is not only the voice of conscience telling a man what is good and what is evil, in addition it keep on nag him saying, "You have committed this sin." More powerfully, this voice influences visible and invisible powers to exact unlawful vengeance on the holder of Dead-Karma. This is the voice that speaks to punish sinners both on Earth and in Hell. So the remover of the Dead-Karma also should be a voice made of spirit.

What is the nature of Dead-Karma: When a man sins, Dead-Karma appears in his conscience, and after appropriate punishment, the Dead-Karma is automatically deleted forever.

The Demands of Dead-Karma to be defaced: The Dead-Karma punishes the body of the sinful man on earth and also drags his soul to hell and punishes the soul there until it dies. Dead-Karma is strong. Please look into what are the demands of power of Dead-Karma (Dead-Works):

If a man fails to respect the by-laws of the conscience, the Dead-Karma will continue to punish and kills that man on the earth. **As per Dead-Karma every man should be punished and die on the earth.**

We've seen in the previous chapters that when a person is punished in the flesh, his soul is untouched. Therefore, the soul which has Dead-Karma should continue to be punished to death in the hell. **As per Dead-Karma every man's soul should be punished and die in the hell.**

The Formula To Remove Dead-Karma

What should be the nature of the Remover to destroy Dead-Karma?:

It is proverb which says "Thorns must be taken out with thorns" Dead-Karma demands a man to suffer punishment and die as per its law. When the evidence is produced with the witness, Dead-Karma which is in the court of conscience will automatically disappear.

All human beings should be punished and die for their dead-karma (sin). What does it mean to be punished and die? If the sinner dies, he won't be there at all! Dead-karma in conscience knows only to carry out the law and not to save man. What is the only way for this?

Since Jesus Christ carried everyone's Dead-Karma (sin) upon himself, all the voices of Dead-Karma (sin) were raised against the Lord Jesus. And everyone's Dead-Karma exacted the most severe punishment on Jesus, killing him once and for all. He shed his precious blood to be a better witness and to produce evidences in every man's conscience.

This blood (Hero) speaks in a very best way inside every man's conscience and produces the evidences for the punishment received and death occurred. In the following sections we will see in detail how the blood of Jesus Christ is powerful and how it washes the dead-karma of conscience.

THE LEGENDARY BLOOD

The cross shows us the seriousness of our sin –

but it also shows us the immeasurable love of God

-Billy Graham

Lust's passion will be served;

it demands, it militates, it tyrannizes

- Marquis de Sade

Before his crucifixion, Jesus' blood did not have the ability to cleanse people's sins. It was through the process of crucifixion itself that his blood gained this power. His blood gained its potency through the suffering and ultimate sacrifice of death on the cross. This blood, metaphorically speaking, has a voice—a voice that echoes the agony and sacrifice endured; a voice that resonates within the conscience of every believer. This voice serves as a testament to the profound significance of Jesus' sacrifice, speaking volumes in the inner chambers of believers' hearts and souls. Jesus suffered and died as per the demands of cruel laws of karma.

Law Of Dead-Karma - 01: Punish The Flesh

The person who has died carrying Evil-Dead-Karma must be punished in the flesh on the earth continuously: Jesus Christ was punished in this world for the Dead-Karma (sins) of everyone and fulfilled the first demand of the law of Dead-Karma.

John 1:29 The next day John seeth Jesus coming unto him, and saith, Behold the Lamb of God, which taketh away the sin of the world.

Isaiah 53:5 But he was wounded for our transgressions, he was bruised for our iniquities: the chastisement of our peace was upon him; and with his stripes we are healed.

Law Of Dead-Karma - 02: Kill The Flesh

Since death is the end of this punishment, the one who has the Dead-Karma must die in the flesh: Jesus Christ was punished and died for every sin of every human being. thus, He fulfilled the second law of Dead-Karma.

Not the sin, Jesus Christ clothed the sinner upon himself and had been punished for our sins: Man's sinful feelings originate in his fleshly body. It is the flesh of man which makes the sinful man. This sinful man must be punished. Jesus Christ clothed upon Him the sinful man of every human being.

Galatians 3:13 Christ hath redeemed us from the curse of the law, being made a curse for us: for it is written, Cursed is every one that hangeth on a tree:

Martin Luther's commentary on Galatians 3:13 explain like this:

"Christ took upon Himself our sins, not by constraint, but of His own good will, in order to bear the punishment and wrath of God: not for the sake of His own person (which was just invincible, and was not in any way guilty), but for our person. So by means of a joyous substitution, He took upon Himself our sinful person and gave to us His innocent and victorious person: with which we, being now clothed, are free from the curse of the law. . . . By faith alone, therefore, we are made righteous, for faith alone lays hold of this victory of Christ." (Martin Luther's commentary on Galatians 3:13)

Just as sinful men clothe on the righteous Jesus Christ upon them and become righteous; similarly, the righteous Jesus Christ who knew no sin clothed sinful people upon himself and was made sin for us.

2Corinthians 5:21 For he hath made him to be sin for us, who knew no sin; that we might be made the righteousness of God in him.

John Calvin's commentary on 2Corinthians 5:21

(John Calvin's commentary and Martin Luther's commentary are similar)

"How can we become righteous before God? In the same way, Christ became a sinner. For He took, as it were, our person, that He might be the offender in our name and thus, might be reckoned a sinner, not because of His own offenses but because of those of others since He

Himself was pure and free from every fault and bore the penalty that was our due and not His own. Now in the same way we are righteous in Him, not because we've satisfied God's judgment by our own works, but because we are judged in relation to Christ's righteousness which we've put on by faith, that it may become our own." (Commentary on 2 Cor. 5:21)

According to the rules of karma, all sinners must be punished. Jesus, the Messiah clothed every sinful person of the world upon Him. The Messiah was punished exactly like punishing a sinful man.

Law Of Dead-Karma - 03: **Punish And Kill The Head**

Sinful thoughts are coming from the head. Since the Messiah carried the sin (dead-karma) of every sinful man in his body, He was made to wear the crown of thorns on His head. The head of Jesus Christ was severely wounded for every sinful thought of man. He was badly punished by Dead-Karma. Messiah suffered and died to destroy the sin of every man's head.

Note: Blood was also shed in this incident. The blood of the Messiah recorded this incident as a witness to produce in the court of human conscience.

Law Of Dead-Karma - 04: **Punish And Kill The Mind**

Luke 22:44 states that Jesus Christ fell into great agony in the garden of Gethsemane. This pain is not caused by the pain of the body, but by the pain of the mind. Blood and sweat come only when human beings experience unbearable pain in the mind. In medical science, blood sweat is called hematidrosis.

Blood sweat is also known as hematidrosis in medicine. It is a rare occurrence in humans. Blood sweats can occur when there is unbearable stress highest. When stress is at its peak, blood begins to leak out of the body. This bleeding will be as thin as water. But the blood of the Messiah was thick, not thin. It was thick enough so that the blood of the Messiah can fell to the ground great drop.

Luke 22:44 And being in an agony he prayed more earnestly: and his sweat was as it were great drops of blood falling down to the ground.

Why there were great drops of blood fell down from Jesus as sweat? Jesus clothed upon him the sinful persons, so, there must have been a great stress than the body had ever seen. Jesus suffered the stress of men. The stress of the Messiah must have been unmanageable. So the angels comforted the Messiah. He was convicted for clothing upon every sinful man.

Note: Blood was also shed in this incident. The blood of the Messiah recorded this incident as a witness to produce in the court of human conscience. Blood sweat shed by Messiah with high stress testifies that it has the ability to relieve the stress caused by Dead-Karma (sin).

Law Of Dead-Karma - 05: **Punish And Kill The Heart**

The heart is the place where the sins of man are approved. Jesus Christ died after His heart was severely punished for the sin of everyone's heart. The sinful thoughts that come out of the head come to the heart to be accepted. Sins are recognized by the heart and the heart commands the body to complete sin. Therefore, the heart of every man must be punished.

Mat 15:19-20 For out of the heart proceed evil thoughts, murders, adulteries, fornications, thefts, false witness, blasphemies: These are the things which defile a man: but to eat with unwashen hands defileth not a man.

Jesus, the Messiah, accepted all those punishments upon Himself. The Messiah's heart was beating heavily with grief and bloodshed. The Messiah was punished by the pains of the mind and by the torments of the flesh. The heart stopped and He died. Then, the heart of the Messiah was pierced with a spear. The heart of Jesus Christ was pierced so that the bloodshed from Him can receive nature to destroy the Dead-Karma from every human's heart.

Note: Blood was also shed in this incident. The blood of the Messiah recorded this incident as a witness to produce in the court of human conscience.

Law Of Dead-Karma - 06: Punish And Kill The Skin

Man's sinful feelings depart from the body. Therefore, Messiah was punished throughout His body and died for the sinful feelings of everyone's body. The scourge which was used by Roman soldiers to beat Messiah had holdings of metal balls and sharp bones. Messiah was scourged thirty-nine times by the mighty Roman soldiers. When the beating hits the entire body, the nerves must have been exposed, the ligaments must have been cut off, and the stomach muscles must have been torn apart. Too much blood must have been shed while doing this. The outer body of Jesus Christ has been torn apart for the sins committed in every human body. Thus, Jesus Christ, the Messiah, suffered the penalties of sin (dead-karma).

Note: Blood was also shed in this incident. The blood of the Messiah recorded this incident as a witness to produce in the court of human conscience.

Law Of Dead-Karma - 07: **Punish And Kill The Hands**

It is the hand of man which comes first to activate sin by actions. So Jesus' hands were severely punished for the sin that every man committed by hands, and Jesus died. The scourge that the Romans used consisted of broken bones and iron balls. With such a whip they struck the hands of the Messiah. For the sinful hands of men, the hands of the Messiah were beaten and nailed to the cross. When Messiah was crucified, about 80 Kilograms of the body weight hung on nails and the nails compressed and tore muscles and nerves of the hands. The torn hands trembled with a sharp pain as the body hung. The Messiah's hands were punished in this way. Thus, Jesus Christ, the Messiah, suffered the penalties of sin (dead-karma).

Note: Blood was also shed in this incident. The blood of the Messiah recorded this incident as a witness to produce in the court of human conscience.

Law Of Dead-Karma - 08: **Punish And Kill The Legs**

The legs of men flame for sin. Since Jesus was clothed with every sinful person of the world, His legs were severely punished for the sin that every man committed on their legs. The Messiah's legs were scourged with broken bones and iron balls. The feet of the Messiah were nailed to the cross. The body weight was also applied to the feet which were nailed to the cross. The body weight on the nailed feet sharpened the pain and caused the legs to suffer severely. The torn feet and entire body trembled together for a few hours. The legs of the Messiah were punished in such a way as to destroy the sin (dead-karma) that humans have done with their feet.

Note: Blood was shed in this incident too. The blood of the Messiah recorded this incident as a witness to produce in the court of human conscience.

Law Of Dead-Karma - 09: **Punish And Kill The Head**

The curse of every man's ancestors was terrible. Jesus Christ also carried the curse of everyone's forefathers on his head. The curse comes from sin. The first curse also came from the first sin (First Dead-karma). Adam and Eve, who carried the curse, became poisonous seeds. The reason is that they carried the curse because of sin. All human beings are not only punished for their sin but also for the curses of Adam and Eve. When the Messiah fell to be punished, he was hanged on the cross. There is a proverb saying, "Cursed is everyone who is hung on a pole" Jesus Christ was punished for the curse of all mankind's ancestors and died.

Galatians 3:13 Christ hath redeemed us from the curse of the law, being made a curse for us: for it is written, Cursed is every one that hangeth on a tree:

Hebrews 9:28 So Christ was once offered to bear the sins of many; and unto them that look for him shall he appear the second time without sin unto salvation.

Hebrews 10:10 By the which will we are sanctified through the offering of the body of Jesus Christ once for all.

Note: Blood was also shed in this incident too. The blood of the Messiah recorded this incident as a witness to produce in the court of human conscience.

STUNNING PROPHECIES

Various religions across the world offered a variety of animal sacrifices and offerings to their gods. However, we cannot observe nature's response to any other sacrifice or offering as they did to the Messiah's sacrifice. Dozens of prophets predicted the Messiah's arrival thousands of years ago, and the Messiah's sacrifice took place in the world history. The non-Christian world also confirms this history. Approximately 365 prophesies regarding the Messiah and his sacrifice have been penned. They all happened in the life of Jesus Christ. No other sacrifice is as significant to humanity as the messiah. Here are various prophetic prophesies concerning the Messiah.

No	List of some Prophecies about Messiah	Fulfilled prophecies
1	It is written that the Messiah would be "a	Jesus Christ was born as a sacrificing life" (John 1:29,

	sacrificing life" (Genesis 22: 8).	Romans 8: 3-4, 1 Corinthians 5: 7)
2	In the Jewish book, it is written that the Messiah would be born on the Virgin (Isaiah 7:14; Genesis. 3:15)	Jesus Christ, the Messiah, was born of the Virgin Mary (Galatians 4: 4-5; Matthew 1:18). Verses 20-21 Islamic scripture, chapter 19 (Surat Maryam), say that the Messiah Jesus was born of the Virgin Mary.
3	It is written that the Messiah would be born of a woman's seed (Genesis 3:15).	Naturally, woman alone does not have seed without male support. The seed of the woman means that the Messiah will be born in the Virgin's womb. Jesus Christ was born in the womb of the virgin (Luke 1: 34-35). This is outside of nature.
4	In the Jewish book, it is written that the Messiah would establish the New Covenant (Jeremiah 31:31)	The Messiah, Jesus, made the New Covenant by His death (Matthew 26:28, Mark 14:24, Luke 22:20, 1 Corinthians 11:25, 2 Corinthians 3:25). (Hebrews 8: 6–13, 9:15, 12:24)

5	In the Jewish religious book, it is written that the Messiah would be abandoned and punished, but he would be called righteous (Ps. 22: 1–31)	Jesus, the Messiah, was abandoned, punished, and finally judged by public that He was righteous (Matthew 27:39, 27: 43–44, 27:46, Mark 15:34, John 19:24, Hebrews 2:12)
6	In the Jewish book, it is written that the Messiah would be rejected and then He will become a corner stone (Ps. 118: 22–24).	Jesus Christ, the Messiah, was rejected by the Israelites. In the year 70 CE, the help of the Messianic Christians was a major help for the Israelites to come together as a nation. The Messiah himself became the corner stone for the nation, Israel (Acts 4: 9–12; Ephesians 2:20; 1 Peter 2: 6-8). Even in the last days Messiah would be the cornerstone for the Israelites
7	In the Jewish book, it is written that the time of the coming of the Messiah to be sacrificed for men will be like this (Daniel 9: 24–27).	Jesus, the Messiah, was sacrificed at the same time mentioned by the prophets (Matthew 24: 15–16, Mark 13: 14–15, Galatians 4: 4)
8	In the Jewish book, it is written that the Messiah would be pierced	Jesus, the Messiah, was pierced (Matthew 24:30;

	(Zechariah 12:10).	John 19: 31–37; Rev. 1: 7)
9	In the Jewish book, it is written that he would be betrayed to death for 30 pieces of silver (Zechariah 11: 12-13).	Jesus, the Messiah, was betrayed to death for 30 pieces of silver (Matthew 26: 14–15, 27: 3, 27: 9–10)
10	In the Jewish religious book, it is written that the Messiah would be lifted up to death (Numbers 21: 6-9)	Jesus, the Messiah, was lifted on the cross and hanged on the cross (John 3: 14–18, Luke 1:50, Luke 1:58, Luke 1:68)
11	It is written that the bones of the Messiah will not be broken (Exodus 12:46).	Jesus' bones were not broken when He died (John 19: 32-33)
12	It is written, "He shall rise from death and be enthroned as King (Psalm 2: 7)."	He rose from the dead and was crowned as a King (Acts 13: 30-33; Romans 1: 3-4)
14	It is written that the Messiah will rise from the dead (Psalm 16: 8-10).	The Messiah was raised from the dead (Matthew 28: 6; Acts 2: 25-32)

15	It is written that Messiah will not see destruction (Psalm 16: 8-10).	The Messiah did not see destruction (Acts 13: 35-37)
16	It is written, "He will cry to God with tears" (Psalm 22: 1).	He appealed to God with tears (Matthew 27:46)
17	It is written that God will abandon the Messiah at death (Psalm 22: 1)	God abandoned the Messiah at death (Mark 15:34)
18	It is written that the Messiah would be abandoned by his own people (Psalm 22: 6).	His own people abandoned Messiah (Luke 23: 21-23)
19	It is written that the Messiah will be mocked (Psalm 22: 7).	Messiah was mocked at His death (Matthew 27:39)
20	It is written, "No one will join the Messiah in the clutches of death" (Psalm 22:11)	No one joined the Messiah in the clutches of death (Mark 14:50)
21	It is written that they have opened their mouths against the Messiah (Psalm 22:13)	They Opened Their Mouth against the Messiah (Luke 23: 21-23)

22	It is written that the mighty warriors will surround the Messiah (Psalm 22: 12-13)	Mighty Warriors Surrounded the Messiah (Luke 23)
24	It is written that the Messiah would be crucified (Psalm 22:14)	The Messiah Was Crucified (Matthew 27:35)
25	It is written that the Messiah would be thirsty at his death (Psalm 22:15).	Messiah's was thirsty at His Death (John 19:28)
26	It is written that Gentiles will look to the Messiah to death (Psalm 22:16).	Gentiles looked to the Messiah to death (Luke 23:36)
27	It is written that the Jews will look to the Messiah to death (Psalm 22:16).	The Jews Viewed the Messiah to Death (Matthew 27: 41-43)
28	It is written that the hands and feet will be pierced (Psalm 22:16)	Hands and feet were pierced (Matthew 27:38)
29	It is written that the garment of the Messiah would partaken (Psalm 22:18).	They partook of the garment of the Messiah (John 19: 23-24)

30	It is written that the garments of the Messiah will be parted (Psalm 22:18).	The garment of the Messiah was parted (John 19: 23-24)
31	It is written that people will fall when they come near to kill the Messiah (Psalm 27: 2)..	People fell to the ground when they came near to arrest Messiah (John 18: 3-6)
32	It is written, "False witnesses and aggressors rise up against the Messiah" (Psalm 27:12)	Two false witness came forward to accuse Messiah (Mathew 26:60)
33	It is written that the Messiah will be sought many times (Psalm 31:13).	They sought to kill the Messiah many times (Matthew 27: 1)
34	It is written that the Messiah would be hated without cause (Psalm 35:19).	They hated the Messiah without cause (John 18: 19-23, John 15: 24-25)
35	It is written, "The Messiah will say, 'I will deliver my spirit into your hand' (Psalm 38: 13-14)	The Messiah said, "Thy hand will deliver my spirit" (Matthew 26: 62-63)
36	The Messiah would become the life sacrifice for all mankind. (Psalm 40:	The Messiah became the sacrifice of all mankind

	6-8)	(Hebrews 10: 10-13)
37	It is written that the Messiah would be betrayed by his own disciples (Psalm 41: 9).	The Messiah was betrayed by His Own Disciples (Mark 14: 17-18)
38	It is written that the Messiah would be cast down by the Jews (Psalm 69: 8)	The Messiah was cast down by the Jews (John 1:11)
39	It is written that the heart of the Messiah is pierced (Psalm 69:20)	The heart of the Messiah was piersed (John 19:34)
40	It is written that the Messiah would be given a bitter drink (Psalm 69:21)	They gave the Messiah a bitter drink (Matthew 27:34)

As previously stated, Messiah was predicted by more than 365 prophecies. The Messiah is the only one who died for sins and resurrected from the grave. His life-giving substance has the power to eliminate the Dead-Karma. In the next chapters, we'll go through this in depth.

TESTIMONY OF NON-CHRISTIAN DOCUMENTS

Nothing of spiritual significance comes without sacrifice. Your spirituality will always be measured by the size of your sacrifice. - Jerry Falwell

When God becomes a Man and lives as a creature among His own creatures in Palestine, then indeed His life is one of supreme self-sacrifice and leads to Calvary -C.S. Lewis

Not By An Eclipse

When the Messiah died, the earth was shrouded in darkness. Many people believed that the eclipse happened when the Messiah died. However, research indicates that there was no likelihood of a solar eclipse on that day. After analyzing the astronomy of that day, historians have wondered. Passover is observed on the full moon day.

There is no chance of a solar eclipse on this day. Sextus Julius Aprikanus Tallus, a non-Christian historian, writes in a significant historical work, "This darkness calls, as appears to me without reason... For the Hebrews celebrate the Passover on the 14th day according to the moon, and the passion of our Saviour falls on the day before the Passover, but an eclipse of the sun takes place only when the moon comes under the sun." Therefore, when the Messiah was crucified, there was no chance of an eclipse. But on this particular day, the land was shrouded in darkness. What is the source of this darkness? The sun was hidden because it did not want to witness the killing of the Messiah, Jesus Christ. This is the world's greatest miracle. On the earth, nobody could witness such a dreadful response of nature in anyother sacrifice or offerings as it did when Messiah was sacrificed.

Sun Mysteriouly Disappeared

This darkness was also mentioned in the documents of the Romans who killed Christians in clusters. As per this document, "In the same hour, too, the light of day was withdrawn, when the sun at the very time was in his meridian blaze. Those who were not aware that this had been predicted about Christ, no doubt thought it an eclipse. You yourselves have the account of the world-portent still in your archives." says Tertullian, a Roman scholar (A non Christian). The sun was hiding itself, not wanting to see the death of Jesus Christ. This is the greatest miracle and response of nature.

The Stars Were Seen During The Day

Phlegon of Tralles was an ancient Greek writer who was not a Christian. He was a freedman of Hadrian, the Roman Emperor who reigned from 117CE. Phlegon of Tralles wrote about the day of death of Messiah, "it became night in the sixth hour of the day [i. e., noon] so that stars even appeared in the heavens"

Matthew 27:45 Now from the sixth hour there was darkness over all the land unto the ninth hour.

On the earth, nobody could witness such a twinkling stars response of nature in anyother sacrifice or offerings as it did when Messiah was sacrificed.

6.3 Richter Earth Quake

The researchers called Jefferson Williams, Markus Schwab and A. Brauer (2012) from "Supersonic Geophysical, LLC, Los Angeles, CA 90042, USA; GFZ And German Research Centre for Geosciences" gave An International Geology report on "early first-century earthquake in the Dead Sea". These plausible candidates include the earthquake reported in the Gospel of Matthew, an earthquake that occurred sometime at the time of crucifixion of Jesus Christ. It was sufficiently energetic to deform the sediments at Ein Gedi. The authors concluded that a widespread 6.3 magnitude earthquake has been confirmed.

Matthew 27:50-51 Jesus, when he had cried again with a loud voice, yielded up the ghost. And, behold, the veil of the temple was rent in twain from the top to the bottom; and the earth did quake, and the rocks rent;

On the earth, nobody could witness such a ground breaking response of nature in anyother sacrifice or offerings as it did when Messiah was sacrificed.

Earthquake And Darkness

A non Christian, Phlegon of Tralles (Ancient Greek) was a Greek writer, he wrote, "It became night in the sixth hour of the day [i. e., noon] so that stars even appeared in the heavens. There was a great earthquake in Bithynia, and many things were overturned in Nicaea." We cannot see such a response of nature like - earth quake and day darkness at the same time - in any other sacrifice or offerings in the world as it responded when Messiah was sacrificed.

Thickest Screen Was Torn

For themselves, the Israelites built the first Temple. The Temple was constructed around 957 BC. The Babylonians completely destroyed the first Temple. On the remains of the previous Temple, the second Temple was constructed. It was reconstructed around 515 BC. The second Temple era saw the death of the Messiah. The curtain in the Israelite Temple was roughly sixty feet high and four inches thick. The purpose of the Temple curtain was to prevent the unclean people from approaching the presence of God.

The very thick Jewish Temple curtain was torn in two when Jesus Christ gave up his life. There is no longer a need for curtains between God and mankind since the Messiah, Jesus Christ, paid for the sins of the world and made them holy before the Father.

Mat 27:51 And, behold, the veil of the temple was rent in twain from the top to the bottom; and the earth did quake, and the rocks rent;

The great curtain of the Temple was torn apart at the moment of Jesus Christ's death. The barrier that separated people was removed. Nature did not respond in the same way to any other sacrifice or offering in the world as it did when Messiah was sacrificed.

The Rocks Were Parted

At the time of Messiah's death, the rocks were split, tombs were uncovered, and the bodies of numerous saints who had been asleep were resurrected. They rose from the tombs and entered the sacred city, where they were found in large numbers. Jesus Christ's death did not occur in a remote nook. The heavens, the sun, the government, common people, and His disciples all saw his death. When they saw the earthquake and what transpired, they exclaimed, "Truly, this is the Son of God." The Centurion and those who were guarding Jesus were terrified. On the earth, nobody could witness such a rending rock response of nature in anyother sacrifice or offerings as it did when Messiah was sacrificed.

The Messiah's living blood (hero) contained life, power, and the ability to eradicate the Dead-Karma from everyone's conscience. In the next chapters, we will see more about the working method of the blood of Jesus Christ in everyone's conscience.

***

Evidence From The Jewish Writer Josephus (Jews Opposed Jesus As Messiah)

The Jews killed the Messiah, Jesus Christ. Jews were the ones who persecuted Christian men and women, inflicted harsh punishments on them, humiliated and murdered. As religious extremists, Jews demolished Christian churches. In the Roman Empire, there was a

Jewish historian named Josephus who was not a Christian. He belongs to the Jewish faith. His mother was a Jewish priest's daughter. He was a member of the royal family. Josephus was no ordinary historian. In the first century, he was a Roman-Jewish scholar. The Judeo-Messianic prophecies, according to Josephus, were the catalyst for the start of the first Roman-Jewish conflict. When Vespasian became Emperor in 69 AD, he elevated Josephus to a position of prominence in his realm. Josephus was awarded Roman citizenship.

Josephus was later re-named "Flavius Josephus" after the Roman sovereign of Flavius. It is worth noting that following this Emperor Vespasian, Josephus became an advisor and friend of Vespasian's son Titus, a Roman emperor. Emperor Titus' translator during the conquest of Jerusalem was Josephus. The second Temple of the Israelites, completed during Herod's reign, was looted and destroyed. The Israelites were still unable to build the Temple there after over two thousand years.

Josephus wrote not only the history of the first Jewish-Roman war from 66 BC to 70 AD and the history of war of the Jews in 75 AD, he also wrote the Antiquities of the Jews. The actual details of death of Jesus Christ on the cross have been recorded by him about two thousand years ago. Please note what he had written about Jesus Christ:

"At this time there appeared Jesus, a wise man, for he was a doer of astounding deeds, a teacher of people who receive the truth gladly. He won a following both among many Jews and among many of Greek origin. When Pilate, because of an accusation made by our leaders, condemned him to the cross, those who had loved him previously did not cease to do so. Up until this very day the tribe of Christians (named after him) has not died out."

Evidence Given By Tacitus The Professor Of History Of The Roman Kingdom

Augustus was the first Commander of War in the Roman Empire in the first century, and he eventually became the Roman Empire's first Emperor. He controlled the Roman Empire from January 16, 27 BC to August 20, 14 AD. This Augustus was captured by Emperor Tiberius. King Claudius and King Nero succeeded him as rulers of the Roman Empire. Tacitus, a well-known Roman historian, had written two volumes on the lives of these four emperors: Augustus, Tiberius, Claudius, and Nero. Tacitus was a devoted member of the Roman Empire's political establishment. Tacitus was allowed permission to investigate what the Romans were discussing in Parliament and to publish the records of the Roman Senate. Tacitus is often recognised as one of the finest Roman historians of the modern era. According to historian Ronald Mellor, the Annals are "Tacitus' finest work" and the "Pinnacle of Romance Writing."

The Roman historian Tacitus wrote in his Annals about the death of Jesus Christ like this, "Christus, from whom their name [Christians] is derived, was executed at the hands of the procurator Pontius Pilate in the reign of Tiberius..."

Tacitus has clearly written the truth of Jesus Christ's death and confirmed that Jesus Christ was crucified in the Roman Empire. The non-Christian version has confirmed the crucifixion of Jesus Christ.

Tacitus also states in his autobiography that the city of Rome was set on fire by Nero targeting Christians.

When he wrote about Jesus Christ, Tacitus was the governor of the province of Asia, and as a member of the inner circle in Rome he would have known of the official position with respect to the fire and the Christians (Jesus & the Rise of Early Christianity: A History of New Testament Times by Paul Barnett 2002 ISBN 0-8308-2699-8 page 30)

The Evidence Of Letter Of Mara Bar

Mara bar, Serapion's son, is also written Mara bar. Sarapion was a Stoic philosopher from Syria in the Roman Empire. He was remembered for a letter he sent in Syriac to his son, Serapion (his son's name also same as Father's). The letter was written after 73 AD but before the 3rd century, with most academics placing it shortly after 73 AD within the first century. The text might be an early non-Christian reference to Jesus' crucifixion. The letter refers to the unjust treatment of "three wise men": the murder of Socrates, the burning of Pythagoras, and the execution of "the wise king" of the Jews. In this passage the author explains that when the wise are oppressed, not only does their wisdom triumph in the end, but God also punishes their oppressors

Evidences In Babylonian Talmud

It is also written in Babylonian Talmud (Sanhedrin 43a, Soncino Edition) about crucifixtion of Jesus Christ, “On the eve of the Passover Yeshu was hanged. For forty days before the execution took place, a herald went forth and cried, 'He is going forth to be stoned because he has practiced sorcery and enticed Israel to apostasy. Anyone who can say anything in his favor let him come forward and plead on his behalf.' But since nothing was brought forward in his favour he was hanged on the eve of the Passover!"

STRUCTURING THE REMOVAL OF SIN

What can wash away my sin?

Nothing but the blood of Jesus;

What can make me whole again?

Nothing but the blood of Jesus

-Robert Lowry

Destruction of Dead-work means the destruction of Dead-Karma. The right witnesses defuse all the crimes in court. Man will be acquitted by the right witnesses. When the animals were sacrificed, their blood was sprinkled in man's conscience where Dead-Karma is active. The blood of animals begins to argue in the conscience to eradicate a man's Dead-Karma. It is only during this argument that the horror of the Dead-Karma is temporarily calmed down. But the testimony of the blood of the animals that was sacrificed for sin is weak and inadequate. So the testimony of that blood is soon rejected. What is the reason for this? Dead-Karma's revenge is that only man should be punished and killed, not animal. Animals cannot be punished in accordance with the sins made by human minds, hearts, acts, and emotions. But how, more than anything else, did the blood of Jesus become a three-dimensional witness to liberate man from Dead-Karma? The blood, the Spirit, and the water in the blood of Jesus Christ have all become powerful testimonies.

1John 5:8 And there are three that bear witness in earth, the Spirit, and the water, and the blood: and these three agree in one.

Spirit, water, and blood cells are all combined to form blood. In the blood, the water, the spirit, and the blood cells are united together as one, just as the Father, the Son, and the Holy Spirit are one. Three substances of blood provide a strong testimony in the court of conscience. We'll examine in depth how the evidence provided by the blood of Jesus Christ is flawless, powerful, and reliable in destroying Dead-Karma.

Everyone knows that conscience speaks. Conscience makes the law. In case, if anyone stands against its law, conscience justifies that it is a crime.

Romans 2:15 Which shew the work of the law written in their hearts, their conscience also bearing witness, and their thoughts the mean while accusing or else excusing one another;

Thus, the conscience speaks to both make and question about justice. Their conscience is the legislation and the court of mankind.

Blood Gives Its Testimony To The Judge

Blood has a voice. Forensic science is one of the branches of modern science. Forensic science revealed that there is a voice in the blood after research. Forensic science investigates the voice of the blood. That voice has the ability to speak about criminal's activity. Even if the criminals do not speak with their tongues, the blood of the criminal speaks about them and betrays them. Just recently, forensic research has revealed that blood has the ability to speak. However, it is recorded properly approximately 3500 years ago in the Holy Bible that blood can speak. The cry of Abel's blood to God is not just fiction or fantasy; it is scientifically shown to be true.

Genesis 4:10 And he said, What hast thou done? the voice of thy brother's blood crieth unto me from the ground.

The Bible states that man's blood has a voice, and forensic science has confirmed this. The blood of Jesus accurately recorded every pain of Jesus Christ so that it could produce its powerful voice in the court of conscience to deface every sin (dead-karma). When Jesus' blood is sprinkled on man's conscience, the blood testifies in the court of conscience and liberates mankind from all sins.

Hebrews 9:14 How much more shall the blood of Christ, who through the eternal Spirit offered himself without spot to God, purge your conscience from dead works to serve the living God?

Water Gives Its Testimony To The Judge

The conscience does not easily agree with anything until it is flawless. Despite the fact that the animals were sacrificed, the conscience will continue to nag the sinner. Even if a man contributes to charity, his conscience will plague him. It will continue to punish sinners. What exactly does a guilty conscience demand? The sinner must be punished and killed! This is the ultimate demand. We've seen how Jesus Christ, who took on the form of our sinful man, was punished for our sins, bled, and died. Blood serves as testimony for the punishments that

Jesus endured. But what proof do we've that Jesus Christ died? The water provides proof for death Jesus Christ since it came out of his dead body along with His blood. This is the reason Christian water immersion (Baptism part-1) signifies death and rising from the water (Baptism part-2) signifies the resurrection.

Before dying, Jesus Christ hung on the cross for several hours. His heart ought to have been racing quickly at this hour. Medically speaking, Jesus' body experienced "hypovolemic shock" since there was a minimum amount of blood and also other body fluid losses. The lack of blood in a person's body results in hypovolemic shock. As a result, water must have accumulated around Jesus' heart and lungs. Pericardial effusion refers to the accumulation of water surrounding the heart. When a Roman soldier stabbed Jesus in the side, blood and water gushed out because Jesus had pericardial effusion.

John 19:33 But when they came to Jesus, and saw that he was dead already, they brake not his legs: But one of the soldiers with a spear pierced his side, and forthwith came there out blood and water.

During sacrifice, even animals do not die from such suffering. Animals die in just a few minutes. But only Jesus endured the long, excruciatingly painful process of dying on the cross for our sins. The water from Jesus' body also confirms that Jesus Christ died. Blood of Jesus Christ came to testify in sinner's conscience with water.

1John 5:6 This is he that came by water and blood, even Jesus Christ; not by water only, but by water and blood. And it is the Spirit that beareth witness, because the Spirit is truth.

Jesus Christ's blood and water serve as witnesses and convey the proof. In the court of conscience, Jesus' blood and the water testify that Jesus was punished for all kinds of sins committed against the court of human conscience.

> *Hebrews 9:14 How much more shall the blood of Christ, who through the eternal Spirit offered himself without spot to God, purge your conscience from dead works to serve the living God?*

Note: Water gives witness to Jesus' death. Every man is required to go through baptism process in order to symbolise both Jesus' death to sin and his resurrection to justice.

The Spirit Gives Its Testimony To The Judge

The spirit in Jesus Christ's blood is more unique than the spirits of humans and animals in this world. Having an eternal Spirit is unique. Nobody can defeat the eternal Spirit. Nobody can kill or break the eternal Spirit. That is why it is referred to as the eternal Spirit. The eternal Spirit is a reference to God. Nobody can stand up to the eternal Spirit. The accusing spirit formed in the conscience cannot stand up to God's eternal Spirit. It will undoubtedly cleanse your conscience with the eternal Spirit found in Jesus Christ's blood!

> *Hebrews 9:14 How much more shall the blood of Christ, who through the eternal Spirit offered himself without spot to God, purge your conscience from dead works to serve the living God?*

Blood testifies that Jesus was punished for our sins. Water testifies that Jesus died for our sins. The persons who are washed by the blood and water of Jesus Christ are the saved ones. The eternal spirit of the Messiah testifies in the court of saved man's conscience that he is the child of God. And the same Spirit testifies that the seed of God is present in such a man. With these three witnesses, the Dead-Karma in the conscience of man disappears.

When the blood of Jesus Christ is sprinkled on the conscience of a person by faith, the blood of Jesus, knowing the cruel sound of man's conscience, will not remain silent. The blood of Jesus Christ shall wash away all the Dead-Karma (sin) that has stained the conscience, stating that Jesus Christ suffered all the terrible consequences of this person's sin and died. Whatever their sins are, no matter how big or small, the blood of Jesus Christ has all the power to cleanse them all.

1John 1:7 But if we walk in the light, as he is in the light, we've fellowship one with another, and the blood of Jesus Christ his Son cleanseth us from all sin.

The Structured Cleaning Of Conscience

Just as the Father, the Son, and the Holy Spirit are embedded as one and the blood, the water, and the spirit are embedded as one to be a perfect witness.

1John 5:8 And there are three that bear witness in earth, the Spirit, and the water, and the blood: and these three agree in one.

The testimony of all three in the court of conscience is fabulous and flawless. The testimony of the Messiah's holy blood, the eternal Spirit, and the water of Jesus is perfect, powerful, and authoritative.

Hebrews 9:14 How much more shall the blood of Christ, who through the eternal Spirit offered himself without spot to God, purge your conscience from dead works to serve the living God?

How To Use Communion To Remove Dead-Karma

Small feelings of guilt had been bothering me for a few months. That was simply bullying. In my conscience, I prayed with the blood of Jesus Christ, saying, "Jesus, wash me with your blood." Nonetheless, that sense of guilt continued to harm me. When we feel guilty, it means that our sin has not been washed away. Because the atrocity of the Dead-karma is still ruling in conscience, I was afraid that my guilty conscience would nag and condemn me. I was reading 1 Corinthians chapter 11 one day. Some of the verses were particularly moving to me. The secret of how to use the blood of Jesus Christ to cleanse our sins from our conscience was revealed to the apostle Paul by the Lord.I have summarized the procedure for cleaning the dead works (sin) from the conscience while taking part in the Holy Communion below.

Warning: Do not eat the bread (communion) with hungry, or hasty mood (1 Corinthians 11: 20-21).

Examine yourself: Examine yourself and participate in the Lord's Supper (1 Corinthians 11: 20-21). Before eating the body of the Lord and drinking the blood, you must examine what kind of person you are and what sins are in you (1 Corinthians 11:28).

Confess your sins: Don't hide your sins to God. You must confess and expose your sins to God. When you open up the conscience to expose your hidden sins, it will be brought to the surface. No one should hide the sins. If you don't confess your sins, your sin will plague you inside (Proverbs 28:13). Why should open up your sins? You have to open up the sins so that it can hear the witnesses of the blood, the water and the spirit of the Lord.

Proclaim the death of the Lord: What is the purpose of the communion? Proclaiming the death of the Lord is the purpose of the communion (1 Corinthians 11: 23-25). How should we proclaim the death of the Lord? We have to meditate on the sufferings and death of the Lord while taking part in the communion; this is the way to proclaim the Lord's death (1 Corinthians 11:26). In doing so, your conscience records the sufferings and the death of Jesus Christ and washes away Dead-Works (sins) from your conscience.

When should you eat bread?: Say these things to the Lord Jesus Christ and declare, "You have been scourged for my sins, for my lies, for misleading others, for not doing good, for not disobeying, etc." Meditate about how deeply Jesus was wounded for your worst sins. When you say this, your conscience's dead-karma (sin) is listening. Your conscience will begin to feel that Jesus' body was punished for your sins.

… Eat the bread now…

Eat the bread (the body of Jesus) which was beaten for your sins.

When should you drink the blood: **Receive** the wine as the blood of Jesus. This is the blood of the New Covenant. Meditate on the shedding of this blood through Jesus' wounds. While meditating on the blood which passed through the wounds of body of Jesus Christ, tell your conscience so that it can listen to the blood.

1. Roman soldiers wound a crown from thorns and they placed it on the head of Jesus. Meditate on the blood which gushed out of the wounds of Jesus Christ while He was suffering wounds made by crown of thorns. Tell your conscience loud about his suffering for you so that it can listen.

2. Meditate on the blood which gushed out of the wounds while Jesus Christ was pierced through the hands and feet, and also the piercing on the sides. Tell your conscience loud about this suffering for you so that it can listen.
3. Meditate the blood which gushed out of the wounds while Jesus Christ was scourged thirty nine times. Each time there were dozens of wounds on His body. Tell your conscience loud about this suffering for you so that it can listen.
4. Likewise, meditate and tell your conscience loud about the hanging on the cross, carrying the cross, the blood sweat of Jesus Christ etc.,

People do not know how deeply a man is wounded immediately after an injury. However, even in the case of a minor wound, the blood contains the necessary healing ingredients. How is that possible? It is possible because only the blood can determine the depth of a wound. The depth of the wound is discerned by blood. If an injury is severe, blood will flow to the wound in proportion to its depth. Only the blood can tell how deep the wound is and how painful it is. All of Jesus Christ's sufferings are accurately known by his blood. The blood of Jesus Christ has stored the information about the wound in order to produce it as evidence in the court of every human being's conscience. If you drink the blood of Jesus in communion, it speaks to your conscience with all the evidences about Jesus Christ's punishment. Then the Dead-Works that are working against you will lose their life, strength, and power. The Dead-Works (Dead-Karma) will be removed from your conscience. Your conscience will be washed clean of the dead works.

… Now drink the communion wine …

Improper Communion Might Go Terribly Wrong!

Everyone has to examine how the body of Jesus was punished for the sin of everyone. It is a crime in the eyes of God to drink the blood of

Jesus as a wordly ritual without meditating on sufferings of Jesus Christ and also not announcing His death. The judgement of God will come upon them.

1Corinthians 11:29 For he that eateth and drinketh unworthily, eateth and drinketh damnation to himself, not discerning the Lord's body.

By this judgment, believers are sick in spirit, soul and body. Many believers died. Please note that this is the death of the believers.

1Corinthians 11:30 For this cause many are weak and sickly among you, and many sleep.

Therefore, regardless of what kind of believer they are, everyone should only use the blood of Jesus Christ to wash away their sins after meditating on how Jesus Christ's body was beaten in exchange for their wrong doings. I was moved by these verses. After I confessed my sins, I observed how Jesus' body was beaten for my sins. My sins were washed away with the blood of the new covenant. The fierceness feeling of my conscience was deleted. I was released. Do not simply say that Jesus will wash away your sins. Wash away your sins according to what St. Paul received from the Lord and be set free.

Every believer when they are newly born again, they will meditate on Jesus' sufferings deeply. They will feel their sin washed away by the blood of Jesus. This must continue until they die physically.

Because the blood of Jesus Christ has completely washed away the Dead-Karma, there will not be any Dead-Karma in the conscience. So hell cannot touch the man who is washed by the blood of the Lamb of God.

❖

The Eucharist And The Response Of Conscience

Transubstantiation is the Catholic belief that during the Eucharist, the bread and wine truly become the body and blood of Jesus Christ. Consubstantiation, associated with Martin Luther, teaches that Christ's body and blood are truly present together with the bread and wine — but their substance remains unchanged; they remain bread and wine.

The Eucharist, also known as Holy Communion, is central to the Christian faith and carries deep spiritual meaning. Yet, Christians have long debated whether the bread and wine are literally Christ's body and blood, or symbolic elements meant to remind us of Him. This ongoing debate has led to divisions among Christian denominations.

Understanding what Jesus taught about Communion — and how it relates to our personal faith and conscience — is essential. Much of the disagreement arises from differing views on the spiritual meaning of Christ's body and blood in the life of a believer. The following sections explore how the Bible and various Christian traditions interpret the Eucharist.

Interpretations Of Communion Among Christian Denominations

1. Catholicism: The Catholic Church teaches that through transubstantiation, the bread and wine become the actual body and blood of Christ. Participation in the Eucharist is seen as a real encounter with Christ's sacrifice, providing divine grace and spiritual nourishment.

2. Orthodox: Christianity: The Orthodox Church also believes the bread and wine become Christ's body and blood, but it describes this transformation as a divine mystery. The emphasis is on the sacramental and sacred reality of the Eucharist, rooted in early Christian tradition.
3. Lutheranism: Lutherans hold to a doctrine called sacramental union. They believe that Christ's body and blood are truly present "in, with, and under" the bread and wine. The elements are not physically changed but are united with Christ's real presence as a means of grace.
4. Reformed: Reformed Christians view the bread and wine as symbols of Christ's body and blood. Christ is spiritually present, not physically. The emphasis is on the symbolic and covenantal meaning of the sacrament.
   Anglicanism: Anglican beliefs vary widely. Some Anglicans hold views similar to Catholicism or Lutheranism, while others take a more symbolic approach. This diversity reflects the broad theological spectrum within the Anglican tradition.
5. Methodist, Baptist, and Pentecostal/Evangelical Traditions These groups generally see the Eucharist as symbolic or commemorative. They emphasize personal faith and remembrance rather than a physical or sacramental transformation.

The Flesh And The Blood – Or Just Remembrance?

The **blood of Christ** works to purge the human conscience from "dead works" so that we may serve the living God. Therefore, believers must present the flesh and blood of Christ in their conscience as the *real* flesh and *real* blood of Christ — through faith.

Hebrews 9:14 – "How much more shall the blood of Christ, who through the eternal Spirit offered himself without spot to God, purge your conscience from dead works to serve the living God?"

Even today, the blood of Christ bears witness within the human conscience.

1 John 5:8 – "There are three that bear record on earth: the Spirit, the water, and the blood; and these three agree in one."

Human conscience must hear this record of the blood through faith. The voice of the blood represents the voice of the person. Therefore, the voice of Christ's blood is the voice of Christ Himself. Hearing this voice by faith is the only way to escape eternal judgment.

Hebrews 12:25 warns: "If they did not escape when they refused Him who spoke on earth, much less shall we escape if we reject Him who speaks from heaven."

The way to escape is to not refuse His voice.

The Communion Of The Body And Blood

Paul affirms that the bread and cup represent true communion with Christ's body and blood:

1 Corinthians 10:16 – "The cup of blessing which we bless, is it not the communion of the blood of Christ? The bread which we break, is it not the communion of the body of Christ?"

He also warns that partaking unworthily is spiritually dangerous:

1 Corinthians 11:27–29 – "Whoever eats this bread or drinks this cup of the Lord unworthily shall be guilty of the body and blood of the Lord... For he that eats and drinks unworthily eats and drinks judgment to himself, not discerning the Lord's body."

Thus, believers must discern and believe that the elements represent the real body and blood of the Lord, while also remembering His suffering. When received in full faith, the real flesh and blood of Christ can cleanse the conscience and silence the "dead voice" of sin.

Faith in the real presence of Christ's flesh and blood is vital. Equally important is remembering His suffering, which together purify the conscience from sin (or "Dead-karma").

Voices From Church Tradition

Martin Luther sais, "It is the true body and blood of our Lord Jesus Christ, in and under the bread and wine, given to us Christians to eat and drink, as instituted by Christ Himself."

Luther emphasized the **sacramental union** — that Christ's body and blood are truly present "in, with, and under" the elements, though not physically transformed.

John Calvin said, "The secret of the sacrament lies in the fact that by the Spirit we are lifted up to Christ in heaven; thus, we feed upon His body and blood."

St. Thomas Aquinas said, "The presence of Christ's true body and blood in this sacrament cannot be detected by sense or understanding, but by faith alone."

Faith And Remembrance

Some denominations take part in Communion merely as a memorial — focusing only on remembrance. However, doing so without faith in the real presence of Christ's flesh and blood can be spiritually dangerous.

If the Eucharist were only symbolic, Christ could have simply asked us to remember Him without the bread and wine. Instead, He gave us the Lord's Supper — both to remember His suffering and to receive His body and blood by faith.

Therefore, we must both believe in the real presence and remember the Lord's suffering, allowing our conscience to be purified by His blood.

JESUS DIED TO REMOVE SINS, NOT TO FORGIVE

The Lord Jesus Christ came to this world for the redemption of the souls. Many Christians do not know the methodical cleansing power of the blood of Jesus Christ. Before death on the cross, Jesus Christ forgave sins of many people. In Matthew 9:2, Jesus forgave the sins of sick of palsy and in Luke 7:48 Jesus forgave the sins of a prostitute. Here, an important question arises as to why should Jesus Christ die on the cross if He could forgive sins?

We've seen that when an animal is sacrificed, this sacrificial system also just cover up the sin, that's it. If someone works for a company and possibly commits a sin against the company, the company will forgive them. However, the conscience of sinners is unaffected. Before death on the cross, Jesus forgave sin of the prostitute. Psalm 85:2 says that forgiveness is just covers up sin, that's it. But the sin is still present under this covering.

Psalms 85:2 Thou hast forgiven the iniquity of thy people, thou hast covered all their sin. Selah.

Psalms 32:1 Blessed is he whose transgression is forgiven, whose sin is covered.

The blood of Jesus does not longer cover sin; it washes away the sins completely and makes a man holy.

Revelation 1:5 And from Jesus Christ, who is the faithful witness, and the first begotten of the dead, and the prince of the kings of the earth. Unto him that loved us, and washed us from our sins in his own blood,

About 600 years ago, before Jesus Christ was born, the prophet Ezekiel had foretold that sins would be completely eliminated.

Ezekiel 33:16 None of the sins that he has committed shall be remembered against him…(ESV)

Psalms 103:12 As far as the east is from the west, so far hath he removed our transgressions from us.

This prophecy was fulfilled only when Jesus died on the cross. Jesus' blood is capable of completely washing away sin (Dead-Karma/Dead-Work) from everyone's conscience. How can a man who feels guilty of sin be God's children? No one who has been forgiven of sin has been adopted as a child of God. Even after the animal sacrifice, no one became a child of God. Even after his charitable works, no one has become a child of God. No one has ever become a child of God after enduring punishments for sin. However, only those who were washed clean by Jesus' blood became children of God. Jesus Christ did not come to this world to forgive sins, but Jesus Christ came to this world to wash away the sins with His blood. Only the blood of Jesus Christ can cleanse us of our sins. Instead of asking Jesus Christ to forgive your sins, ask Him to wash them away with His blood. You will become a child of God when your sins are washed away by the blood of Jesus Christ.

One day I was reading Matthew 26:28. It is written in different translations as follows:

This is my blood of the covenant, which is poured out for many for the forgiveness of sins –New International Version

For this is my blood of the covenant, which is poured out for many for the forgiveness of sins - English Standard Version

These translations disturbed me. Because, I have noticed that there is a slight difference between what I said that Jesus Christ did not come to forgive sin and what is mentioned here in these translations. I was a little hesitant. But when I considered other translation it was right with my understanding. Please note the following translation:

For this is My blood of the new covenant, which is shed for many for the remission of sins - New King James Version

For this is my blood of the covenant, which is shed for many unto remission of sins - English Revised Version

In English translation, half the translators translated the word as "forgiveness" and other half the translators translated the word as "removal or remission". But in the Greek language it is originally written "aphesis hamartia". This means removing sin or healed from sin. So the Bible says that Jesus did not shed his blood for forgiveness of sin, but to remove sin or wash away sin.

Being Cheated By Forgiveness

Forgiveness is nothing but covering of sins. Covering of sins can happen even with the blood of the sacrificed animals. But only the blood of Jesus Christ can wash away your sins. Don't be fooled! If your sins are not washed away, the toxic sinful stains of the dead works in your conscience will stand against you and have the power to send you to hell. No one can become holy if sin is not washed away. And no one can see God unless he is holy.

Hebrews 12:14… and holiness, without which no man shall see the Lord:

It is useless to go to Christian congregations and confess your sins to the priests. Stop asking the priests for forgiveness. It's unnecessary. Go to Jesus and ask Him to wash your sins away by His blood. Your sins will be thoroughly washed. Thus, y our Dead-Karma will be removed, and you will be liberated. Imagine how humiliating it would be to forgive sins without even knowing such an important basic teaching of the Bible!

Are You Clean? Check Your Conscience

The best sleeping pill is a clear conscience — Dada J. P. Vaswani

Wealth and power aren't the most important things in life. What is truly important is to have a clear conscience — Eraldo Banovac

If all the world hated you and believed you wicked, while your own conscience approved of you and absolved you from guilt, you would not be without friends — Charlotte Brontë, Jane Eyre

The sinner's guilty conscience is relentlessly seeking vengeance. It will enter the minds of sinners, accusing them without ceasing and leading them to destruction. Consider men who do not have a guilty conscience. Their faces will be filled with joy. They will be prosperous and have a full and happy life. People with a good conscience, no matter how poor or illiterate they are, will have a clear face. Their lives will be peaceful. There is no one on the planet who does not sin. The joy of those who have been forgiven of their sins is only temporary. Nothing compares to the relief and joy of those who have been washed in the blood of Jesus. There would be no Dead-Karma (sin) in their conscience after the washing of sin. Only the blood of Jesus Christ is capable of cleansing the conscience. Only those with a pure heart can see God (Matthew 5:8)

You Might Miss Out The Great Redemption

1) Jesus washed away the sin of believers and made them righteous

Romans 5:9 Much more then, being now justified by his blood…

2) Through the blood, God redeemed man from the wrath of God

Romans 5:9 Much more then, being now justified by his blood, we shall be saved from wrath through him.

3) Since the sin between man and God is washed away by the blood of Jesus Christ, man came nearer to God

Ephesians 2:13 But now in Christ Jesus ye who sometimes were far off are made nigh by the blood of Christ.

Ephesians 2:18 For through him we both have access by one Spirit unto the Father.

4) The blood of Jesus Christ reconciled men and God

Colosians 1:20 And, having made peace through the blood of his cross, by him to reconcile all things unto himself; by him, I say, whether they be things in earth, or things in heaven.

Ephesians 2:16 And that he might reconcile both unto God in one body by the cross, having slain the enmity thereby:

5) Jesus Christ made a new covenant through His blood

Luke 22:20 Likewise also the cup after supper, saying, This cup is the new testament in my blood, which is shed for you.

Hebrews 10:19-20 Having therefore, brethren, boldness to enter into the holiest by the blood of Jesus, By a new and living way, which he hath consecrated for us, through the veil, that is to say, his flesh;

6) Redemption from the nagging of conscience

In the ancient times, the sacrifice of animals was repeated again and gain for the same sin, because, it could not destroy the Dead-Works (Dead-Karma) which is in conscience (Hebrews 10:2). But there is no need for the conscience prick again and again for the same sin even after a man's sin was washed away by the blood of Jesus Christ. Now man is liberated from legal, social, or political reproaches of conscience.

Hebrews 9:14 How much more shall the blood of Christ, who through the eternal Spirit offered himself without spot to God, purge your conscience from dead works to serve the living God?

7) When blood of Jesus Christ washes away the dead-works (Dead-Karma) in conscience, man gets the courage to enter the Holy Place with a clean conscience.

1Pe 1:18-19 Forasmuch as ye know that ye were not redeemed with corruptible things, as silver and gold, from your vain conversation received by tradition from your fathers; But with the precious blood of Christ, as of a lamb without blemish and without spot:

Why does Only the Soul Enter The Heaven

The flesh of man is not going to enter the kingdom of God, only the soul can enter the kingdom of God.

1Corinthians 15:50 Now this I say, brethren, that flesh and blood cannot inherit the kingdom of God; neither doth corruption inherit incorruption.

Why doesn't the Unborn Soul Enter The Heaven

It is very important to the soul to enter the kingdom of Kingdom of God. Scripture says that only a person born in the Spirit can enter the kingdom of the Spirit God.

John 3:5 Jesus answered, Verily, verily, I say unto thee, Except a man be born of water and of the Spirit, he cannot enter into the kingdom of God.

The soul born in the flesh will not enter the kingdom of God

Why does Only the Spirit Born Souls Enter the Heaven

Water-dwelling fish cannot live on land, and land-dwelling animals cannot live in water. The flesh that lives in the water is distinct from the flesh that lives on the ground. Similarly, the soul born in the sinful flesh and the soul born in the Holy Spirit are distinct. The bodies of the spirit world and the fleshly world are distinct. The soul cannot go to heaven and live in the flesh in which it was born. As a result, that soul is not permitted to enter heaven. Only the true man (soul) born of the Spirit can enter and inherit God's kingdom. Therefore it is very important that every man must be born in the Spirit of God.

PREPARATION FOR RE-ENGINEERING

The mystery of born again physical body: Everyone in this world calculates their age only after they are born from their mother's womb. However, the Chinese calculate their age from the moment they were conceived (born) in the mother's womb. Before the kid is developed in the mother's womb, the womb is empty. The baby is born from the mother's empty womb. This is man's first birth. Then he begins to develop amid the impurity and darkness of his mother's womb.

Within ten months, the baby is born again in this world of light after being released from the darkness of the womb of the mother. If not born within the time frame, the human body will die in that impurity and darkness of the womb of the mother. The human physical body will be born again out of the womb of a mother with caution not to die in impurity and darkness. This is the mystery of birth. It is the re-birth of the physical body. If we completely understand these mysteries mankind can be redeemed from the miseries of life.

The Mystery of Born Again Soul: It is natural for a man to be born in the mother's womb and also it is natural to be born again out of the mother's womb, into the world of light, within ten months. Everyone knows this. But, it is sad that why so many religious leaders and preachers are so ignorant of the born again soul! This is why it was a mystery to Nicodemus, even though he was a great teacher of great religion.

John 3:9 Nicodemus answered and said unto him, How can these things be? Jesus answered and said unto him, Art thou a master of Israel, and knowest not these things?

Just as the human body is born for the first time in the womb of the mother, the soul of man is also born in the flesh of the child in the womb of the mother. Take note of what religions say about the state of the soul of a baby born inside its fleshy body.

Major Religions: Everyone Is Born Wrapped In Sin

Let us examine what Hinduism, Islam, Judaism, and Christianity said about man's birth. Every human soul which is born in this world is born sinner, surrounded by the sin.

1. Judaism: As per Judaism, every man who is born in the womb of the mother is born sinner. Her mother conceives the child in the sin.

Psalms 51:5 Behold, I was shapen in iniquity; and in sin did my mother conceive me.

Psalms 51:5 Behold, I was shapen in iniquity; and in sin did my mother conceive me.

So as per Judaism, the human soul is wrapped in the sin just like a baby's physical body is wrapped by the uterus of the mother.

2. Christianity: As per Christianity, every man who is born in the womb of the mother is born sinner. Her mother conceives the child in the sin.

Romans 3:23 For all have sinned, and come short of the glory of God;

Romans 3:9 What then? are we better than they? No, in no wise: for we've before proved both Jews and Gentiles, that they are all under sin;

So as per Christianity, the human soul is wrapped in the sin just like a baby's physical body is wrapped by the uterus of the mother.

3. Islam: According to the Hadith, the Prophet Mohammed of Islam said, "All the sons of Adam are sinners, but the best of sinners are those who repent often ". If so, all the children born in this world are sinners. This sin begins at birth. No one is holy. We can see the cry of the Mohammed for the sinful nature of man in Quran as follows:.

(Namely) those who say: "Our Lord! we've indeed believed: forgive us then our sins and save us from the agony of the fire." Quran 3: 15–16

If ye (but) eschew the most heinous of the things which ye are forbidden to do We shall expel out of you all the evil in you and admit you to a Gate of great honor - Quran 4: 31

So as per Islam, the human soul is born wrapped in sin just like a baby's physical body is wrapped by the uterus of the mother.

4. Jainism: As per Jainism, Karma (sin) will encompass the souls of those who persecute someone by violence, by lying, by stealing, by without self control or by greed. According to Jainism, when people are born from one birth to the next birth, their soul is wrapped in sin (Dead-Karma) and carries the sin (Dead-Karma) with them to another birth also.

So as per Jainism, the human soul is born in the sin.

5. Hinduism: The principle of Hinduism is that the human soul is born with the Karma (sins) of the old genma (old birth) and that he suffers the karma in this genma (in this birth). Although the doctrine of man's seven genma (seven birth) is an argumentative principle in Hinduism, the Hinduism states that man is born of carrying karma (sin), This Karma is the result of the past life. This karma makes a man to be born again and again as sinners. Hinduism states that Hindus are too tired of this multiple born again with the sin.

Punarapi jananam punarapi maranam,
Punarapi janani jatare sayanam,

Iha samsaare bahu dusthare,
Krupayaa pare pahi murare.

Translation:

Again and again one is born,
And again and again one dies,
And again and again one sleeps in the mother's womb,
Help me to cross,
This limitless sea of Life,Which is uncrossable, my Lord.

(From Bhaja Govindam – Adi Shankaracharya)

Thus, as per Hinduism, the human soul is born in sin.

***

According to all religions, the human soul is born into the womb of the mother with the physical body wrapped in sin . After growing in the womb of the mother, at the time of birth, only the baby's physical body is born again from the mother's womb that was full of darkness and unclean stuffs. But the soul that is living inside the uterus of darkness and unclean stuffs of sin (Karma) is not born. Man's soul is still stuck and struggling in the dark and dirty womb of sin (Karma) even after the birth of the physical body.

All are sinners from birth. Not only this, after birth they also commit sins and become guilty of sin. thus, all are destined to hell. If anyone does not want to be covered in the darkest and dirty uterus of sin, they must be born again out of the uterus of sin (Karma). As long as they are covered in the uterus of sin (Karma), all heavenly realms will be shut to them. That is why Jesus Christ said that everyone must be born again.

John 3:3 Jesus answered and said unto him, Verily, verily, I say unto thee, Except a man be born again, he cannot see the kingdom of God.

We've learned in God-Like Engineering –I that the physical body is not the real man. The soul is the real man. Just as the human body is born again from the mother's womb within ten months, every human soul in the womb of sin must be born again within a time frame (before physical body dies). Otherwise the real man's soul will die in the cruel power of the womb of sin (Karma). This is the death of the real man soul. If the sin still remains in man, he must be born again out of it.

The Birth Of The Body And The Soul Are Similar

Jesus said that born again of soul is exactly like an earthly order.

John 3:7-12 Marvel not that I said unto thee, Ye must be born again. The wind bloweth where it listeth, and thou hearest the sound thereof, but canst not tell whence it cometh, and whither it goeth: so is every one that is born of the Spirit. Nicodemus answered and said unto him, How can these things be? ... If I have told you earthly things, and ye believe not, how shall ye believe, if I tell you of heavenly things?

The human soul, like the human body, should be born again from the mother's womb. In the following passages, we are going to see in detail how the soul and fleshy body are similar procedure to born again event.

Born-again procedure of physical body and soul

(1) **Formed in the Darkness:** The "fleshy body" develops in the dark womb of the mother. Likewise, the soul is formed in the dark womb of sin (Ded-Karma).

(2) **Dwelling in the Darkness:** The human body dwells as a child inside its mother's dark womb. Likewise, the soul also dwells in the dark womb of sin. Jesus Christ appeared as a light to the soul which is in the womb of sin.

Isaiah 9:2 The people that walked in darkness have seen a great light: they that dwell in the land of the shadow of death, upon them hath the light shined.

(3) **Formed in an unclean environment:** Previously, medical experts believed that the baby develops in the mother's womb in a clean environment. However, today's medical experts have discovered that this is incorrect. Medical research has now revealed that the baby in the womb is formed in a dirty environment. Similarly, man's soul is formed in an unclean environment of sin. Physical body of man and the soul have the same nature in born again process.

Psalms 51:5 Behold, I was shapen in iniquity; and in sin did my mother conceive me.

Significance of the Dwelling Period in dirt & darkness:
Man must be born again physically out of mother's womb within ten months. If the baby is in the dark and dirty womb even after the end of pregnancy time, the baby will surely die. Likewise, the soul must be

born again out of the womb of the sin before its time ends. Otherwise the soul will pathetically die in the womb of sin.

John 3:3 Jesus answered and said unto him, Verily, verily, I say unto thee, Except a man be born again, he cannot see the kingdom of God.

Physical body of man and the soul have the same nature in born again process.

(4) **Redeemed from darkness:** All fleshy bodies are redeemed from the darkest womb of the mother to the world of light. Likewise, all the souls must be redeemed from darkest womb of sin to the world of eternal light. Jesus had revealed this mystery that fleshy body is into this physical world. And the soul is born into the world of eternal light (We've seen in the previous chapters that spirit, light and life is the same thing).

John 3:6 That which is born of the flesh is flesh; and that which is born of the Spirit is spirit.

(5) **The unborn status is slavery and born again status is freedom:** Unborn babies in the mother's womb do not have the freedom to stretch their legs and hands like newborn babies. In the uterus, the unborn child resembles a slave and is unable to change its position. The newborn baby, however, is no longer enslaved and has complete freedom to change its posture. Similarly, the unborn soul does not have the same level of freedom as the born-again soul. The posture of the unborn soul resembles that of a slave in the womb of the Dead-Karma. Because the born-again soul has been set free from slavery, it has complete freedom to express itself in God's Kingdom.

Physical body of man and the soul have the same nature in born again process.

(6) **General knowledge about born again in humans**: The fleshy body of child that is in the womb of the mother will be born again to receive a better life. This example is set by God for every soul which is living in the womb of the sin. Every soul must be born again out of the womb of sin for the better life. Babies in their mother's womb have the incredible knowledge of physically born again. Babies in the womb understood the significance of being born again. But it is painful to know that even great wise people do not have this simple knowledge as babies have.

(7) **Cutting the umbilical cord:** Cutting the umbilical cord is a very important part of the baby's birth. The baby which is in the womb of the mother was given food through the umbilical cord. After it is born from the womb of the mother the umbilical cord is cut and removed. Likewise, the soul which is in the womb of sin was given the food through sinful desires of a fleshy body and deadly food of the Dead-Karma (sin). After the soul is born again out of the womb of sin, the umbilical cord (desires of the flesh and deadly food of Dead-Karma) must be cut and removed.

> *Eze 16:4 And as for thy nativity, in the day thou wast born thy navel was not cut, neither wast thou washed in water to supple thee; thou wast not salted at all, nor swaddled at all.*

Physical body of man and the soul have the same nature in born again process.

(8) **Must be washed:** The baby's physical body develops in the dirty environment of the womb. The baby's physical body must be washed as soon as it is born. This is how every human soul lives in a spiritually unclean womb known as sin. The newborn soul, like a newborn baby, must be washed with the blood of Jesus Christ.

> *Ezekiel 16:4 And as for thy nativity, in the day thou wast born thy navel was not cut, neither wast thou washed in water to supple thee; thou wast not salted at all, nor swaddled at all.*

(9) **Receiving the seven rays of light:** the baby is born again from the darkness of the womb of the mother into the world of sunlight. The electromagnetic spectrum of sunlight is divided into seven types (rays). When a baby is newly born, it receives seven different types of rays of light. The newborn baby is filled with these seven types of rays. And the baby begins to develop in the new light world. Similarly, a born-again soul must receive and mature in the seven spirits of God (We've seen in the previous chapters that spirit, light and life is the same thing), as listed below. Isaiah 11: 2 says about the seven Spirits of God. Thay are:

1. The Spirit of the LORD 2. The spirit of wisdom

3. The spirit of understanding 4. The spirit of counsel

5. The spirit of might, 6. The spirit of knowledge 7. The spirit of the fear of the LORD

The Seven Spirits of God's Light Descended on Born-Again Man (Judges 15:14; Ephesians 1:17; 1 Corinthians12: 8; Psalm 119: 130; Acts 1: 8; Judges 1: 7).

(10) **Children of darkness and children of light:** In the dark, the unborn baby is physically blind. However, the baby who is physically born again in the realm of light can see in the sunlight. Only light can activate the retina in the human eye. People can only see through their eyes when the retina is activated. Unborn babies are naturally blind, whereas born again babies are not. Thus, unborn babies are the children of darkness, while born again children are the children of light.

Similarly, unborn-again souls are souls of darkness and are thus, blind. Just as the retina in a physically born again child's eye is activated by light to see the wonders of the light world, the eyes of spiritually born again souls are activated to see the wonders of the spiritual light world.

The soul that does not walk in the Spirit of God (light of God) is in the dark. Children of light are souls who walk in God's Spirit (light).

Galatians 5:25 If we live in the Spirit, let us also walk in the Spirit.

(11) **Baby should drink milk:** Physically newborn baby is thirsty and longs for mother's milk. Similarly, every new-born soul must grow up in God's word, which is the milk of wisdom (1 Peter 2: 2).
(12) **As the baby grows up, it should eat solid food:** As the child grows, it seeks solid food to nourish its physical body. Similarly, every newly born soul must be aware of solid spiritual food in order to nourish the soul (1 Corinthians 3: 2)

Awaitng Dangers For Unborn Again Souls

Those who have been born again in the physical body receive new life. The unborn baby dies in darkness of womb. Likewise, the soul which is born again gets a new life. The real man soul gets new life. This is great good news to the world. The unborn again soul die in the dirty and darkest sin. The kingdom of light is far from them. The womb of the mother becomes a poison to kill its unborn baby which did not born again in the due time. Likewise, the womb of sin (Dead-Karma) is a poison to kill every unborn soul.

Psalms 58:3-4 The wicked are estranged from the womb: they go astray as soon as they be born, speaking lies. Their poison is like the poison of a serpent: they are like the deaf adder that stoppeth her ear;

Giving charity or worshipping God will not change man's sinful nature. Furthermore, by doing so, man will not die to sin and live to righteousness. The born-again person must be washed away by the blood of Jesus, must be sealed by the Holy Spirit, must be made in the likeness of righteousness by that Spirit, and must be born again in the Spirit of God, as well as must walk only by the Spirit of God. When a baby is not born out of mother's womb, it cannot enter the world of light. Similarly, if a soul is still in the womb of sin and is not born again, it cannot enter into the lightful kingdom of God.

John 3:3 Jesus answered and said unto him, Verily, verily, I say unto thee, Except a man be born again, he cannot see the kingdom of God.

This is the preparation for God-like re-engineering in man. No one can build God-Like Engineering in them unless they have this basic. Even if they try to build, it will not sustain.

1 Corinthians 3:10 By the grace God has given me, I laid a foundation as an expert builder, ...Each one must be careful how he builds.

We are going to practice all these in the next levels of God-Like Engineering.

BACK TO THE BLUEPRINT OF CREATION

Re-Engineering Of The Earnest Seal Of The Spirit

The happiest man is he

who learns from nature

the lesson of worship

— Ralph Waldo Emerson, Nature

This book teaches us that every creature contains the divine seal. Because nature carries the God's seal, it is very much a form of worship. The primary goal of men is to reclaim God's seal. We don't know if Adam worshipped God before he sinned. The upholding of this divine seal, however, became the most exquisite form of worship to God because he had received God's flawless seal. God washed our sins with His blood and gave us the Spirit as the seal of God.

1) What is the "Key Seal" of the Spirit? God must have given this key seal of the Spirit to the first man, Adam. This identity was given to demand rights in the Kingdom of God. Now, this

identity is given in the hearts of every person who was born again.

> *2Corinthians 1:21-22 Now he which stablisheth us with you in Christ, and hath anointed us, is God; Who hath also sealed us, and given the earnest of the Spirit in our hearts.*

According to the Bible, the Holy Spirit has been given to us as a seal. The word "earnest" is written in Greek dialect as arrhabn (ἀῤῥαβών-arrhabōn). n) This term refers to an advance payment. You will be sure to buy a house, a place, or a vehicle by signing up with an advance payment. In modern times, the Greeks use this word to refer to the "engagement ring" (ἀῤῥαβών-arrhabōn) worn during a wedding. The word 'earnest (ἀῤῥαβών-arrhabōn)' is a promise given to something that is goin g to be redeemed. What to be redeemed? Man must redeem the seals of God which he lost.

> *Ephesians 4:30 And grieve not the holy Spirit of God, whereby ye are sealed unto the day of redemption. We'll see what happens between the day the earnest of the Spirit was given and the day of redemption. Let us also take into account the significance of these days.*

Who will receive the earnest of the spirit? When should one get the earnest of the spirit? God will not send His "Seal of the Spirit" to unclean places or persons. But He sends it to believers who hear the word of the Gospel of God and are then washed by the blood of the Lord Jesus Christ.

> *Ephesians 1:13 In whom ye also trusted, after that ye heard the word of truth, the gospel of your salvation: in whom also*

after that ye believed, ye were sealed with that holy Spirit of promise,

2) For what purpose is the "earnest spirit" given?
Actually the earnest of the Spirit acts as a hub for accepting and connecting multiple living gifts of God.

a. The earnest Spirit is given to receive the first fruits of God. As long as born again man is alive on this earth with this physical body, goodness, blessings and other seals of the Spirit are available to him as the first fruits.

b. Those who have received the earnest of the Spirit will receive the body of glorious light.

c. Along with these, heavenly fruits such as blessings and goodness are also available to those who have the earnest of the Spirit.

Romans 8:23 And not only they, but ourselves also, which have the firstfruits of the Spirit, even we ourselves groan within ourselves, waiting for the adoption, to wit, the redemption of our body.

The Seal of the Spirit is given to be led by the Spirit. The seed of God leads those born of God's Spirit. Not only to be born of God, man also must be led by God. Those who do not practice the leading of the Spirit of God are not children of God.

Romans 8:14 For as many as are led by the Spirit of God, they are the sons of God.

1John 3:9 Whosoever is born of God doth not commit sin; for his seed remaineth in him: and he cannot sin, because he is born of God.

1Peter 1:23 Being born again, not of corruptible seed, but of incorruptible, by the word of God, which liveth and abideth for ever.

The "Earnest of the Spirit" denotes "the promised one." The Scriptures contain priceless promises to free, protect, bless, and treat men. All of these things are out of the ordinary. They are given to those who have overcome temptation and have triumphed in their faith. All of these promises are priceless. Such promises are made to those who have received the earnest of the Spirit. This earnest of the Spirit seal is given to those who have been branded as worthy of all promises.

Ephesians 1:13 … ye were sealed with that holy Spirit of promise

Re-Engineering Of The Earnest Of The Spirit As "Seed Of God"

After the death on the cross, Jesus Christ washed man's unclean sins with His blood, so man become holy. The holy believers are sealed by the Holy Spirit.

Ephesians 1:13 In whom ye also trusted, after that ye heard the word of truth, the gospel of your salvation: in whom also after that ye believed, ye were sealed with that holy Spirit of promise,

The Seal of the Spirit is Seed of God. If so, the seed of the man is the earnest of the Spirit. The believer is born of God, so the Spirit is seen in him as seed of God. thus, the Spirit genetics began in man. Without Jesus Christ, spiritual genetics would not have been possible, and there would not have been any meaning for spiritual life.

1John 3:9 Whosoever is born of God doth not commit sin; for his seed remaineth in him: and he cannot sin, because he is born of God.

After Jesus' crucifixion, believers are born with the seed of the immortal God: The seed of God was restored to man through the death of Jesus Christ and by the seal of the Holy Spirit. Since God gave the seed of the Spirit, the spiritual genetics were restored to man. This is the foundation of true spiritual life.

If you do not have the Spirit of Christ, you are not Christian: The Spirit of God is the seal that shows that believers belong to God (2 Cor 1: 21-22) .

Ephesians 1:14 Which is the earnest of our inheritance until the redemption of the purchased possession, unto the praise of his glory.

Whoever does not receive the Spirit of Christ is not belong to Christ. Whoever does not receive the Spirit of Jesus Christ, then, is not a Christian. Christians are those who have Christ.

Romans 8:9 But ye are not in the flesh, but in the Spirit, if so be that the Spirit of God dwell in you. Now if any man have not the Spirit of Christ, he is none of his.

Re-Engineering Of The Mark Of Child God

The "earnest of the Spirit" is not an ordinary seal. The Spirit is given as a seal and hub which makes believers to call out to God as "Abba,

Father". So it is also given as the Spirit of the Sonship. The Spirit bears witness with our spirit that we are the children of God.

Romans 8:15 For ye have not received the spirit of bondage again to fear; but ye have received the Spirit of adoption, whereby we cry, Abba, Father.

Romans 8:16 The Spirit itself beareth witness with our spirit, that we are the children of God:

Can you look at somebody else and say 'my father?' As a dialect some can call out. But if any children are not proven in a genetic test, it is certainly not a child of genetics. As long as we've the father's seed, we can own the "father" with the genetic right. We can call out to God as father and celebrate His rights through His seed which is the Spirit of God. Even those who did not receive the seed of the Spirit of God also may call out to God as the Father, but the rights of the father cannot be celebrated. It is a great pleasure for God to be called out by man as "Abba Father", not with the seed of the flesh, but with the seed of God.

John 1:13 Which were born, not of blood, nor of the will of the flesh, nor of the will of man, but of God.

Men began to walk in the Spirit of God. They were also called sons of God.

Romans 8:14 For as many as are led by the Spirit of God, they are the sons of God.

Re-Engineering Of The Mark To Join The Kingdom Of God

John the Baptist preached Jesus Christ as the Lamb of God who carried the sin of the world. John the Baptist was well aware that Jesus Christ would bear the sin of the world and free people from sin; and then, the Holy Spirit would come soon after the people were set free from sin. He believed that the kingdom of God would come back to mankind by the coming of the Holy Spirit. So he preached:

Matthew 3:1-2 In those days came John the Baptist, preaching in the wilderness of Judaea, And saying, Repent ye: for the kingdom of heaven is at hand.

Jesus Christ, who knew that He would die for mankind's sins and sanctify the people; and then, the kingdom of God would come back to mankind by the coming of the Holy Spirit; so too Jesus preached:

Matthew 4:17 From that time Jesus began to preach, and to say, Repent: for the kingdom of heaven is at hand.

Everyone was looking for the kingdom of God. Jesus said that the kingdom of God is in you, because He knew that the arrival and working of Holy Spirit is the kingdom of God.

Luke 17:21-22 Neither shall they say, Lo here! or, lo there! for, behold, the kingdom of God is within you. And he said unto the disciples, The days will come, when ye shall desire to see one of the days of the Son of man, and ye shall not see it.

Matthew 12:28 But if I cast out devils by the Spirit of God, then the kingdom of God is come unto you.

After the sin of Adam, the Holy Spirit was lost in him. So the kingdom of heaven went too far from him. After the Lord Jesus died on the cross and set man free from sin, he gave the Holy Spirit into the heart of man. The Holy Spirit was again poured out on believers (Acts 2: 1-4). The kingdom of heaven has returned. Believers are now near to the kingdom of heaven.

Re-Engineering To Forbid Condemnation

Jesus Christ gave simple and better law to the believers than the Law of Moses. The law is to be led by the Spirit.

> *Galatians 5:18 But if ye be led of the Spirit, ye are not under the law.*

The Mosaic Laws (laws of Moses) did not make any one to become child of God. But the law that was administered by the Holy Spirit made believers children of God. The Law of Moses is the Law of Killing. But the law of the Spirit gives life.

> 2 Corinthians 3:6 Who also hath made us able ministers of the new testament; not of the letter, but of the spirit: for the letter killeth, but the spirit giveth life.

The laws of Moses is the law of death, its glory will vanish. But the Law of the Spirit is immortal glory.

> *2 Corinthians 3:7-8 But if the ministration of death, written and engraven in stones, was glorious, so that the children of Israel could not stedfastly behold the face of Moses for the glory of his countenance; which glory was to be done away: How shall not the ministration of the spirit be rather glorious?*

Re-Engineering Of The Seven Spirits

Through his death, Jesus Christ restored the likeness of God that Adam had lost. This is the primary reason for the coming of Jesus Christ in the flesh.

Luke 19:10 For the Son of man is come to seek and to save that which was lost.

Man is washed with blood of Jesus Christ after hearing the gospel of the Lord Jesus Christ. Then, the Holy Spirit comes and dwells in Him (Romans 8: 9; 1 Corinthians 6: 19-20, 12:13). Immediately after the coming of the Holy Spirit, the seven spirits of God begin to appear in him. Then the man is sealed again by the seven spirits of God.

Man must have the likeness of his Creator. Jesus was filled with the seven Spirits of God. In his vision, the prophet Isaiah saw that the Spirit of the Lord rested upon Jesus Christ.

Isaiah 11:2 And the spirit of the LORD shall rest upon him, the spirit of wisdom and understanding, the spirit of counsel and might, the spirit of knowledge and of the fear of the LORD;

These Spirits were seven. The seven spirits of Jesus Christ are part of the likeness and image of God.

Revelations 1:13 And in the midst of the seven candlesticks one like unto the Son of man, clothed with a garment down to the foot, and girt about the paps with a golden girdle.

Revelations 4:5 And out of the throne proceeded lightnings and thunderings and voices: and there were seven lamps of fire burning before the throne, which are the seven Spirits of God.

We've seen how the seven seals of God are the seven seal of men in the preceding chapter. To have the likeness of his Creator, every man also must have the seven Spirits of God as divine seal on him.

Re-Engineering Of Nine Fruits

Immediately after the coming of the Holy Spirit, the fruits of the Holy Spirit are found in believers. The fruit of such a spirit appears as a seal of God in man. Scripture tells us about the nine fruits of the spirit that sealed man.

Galatians 5:22-23 But the fruit of the Spirit is love, joy, peace, longsuffering, gentleness, goodness, faith, Meekness, temperance: against such there is no law.

The Lord Jesus Christ once again brought back the fruit of the Spirit that Adam lost. The likeness of God was found again in the believers. Jesus Christ redeemed Adam's lost likeness of God.

Luke 19:10 For the Son of man is come to seek and to save that which was lost.

Re-Engineering Of Gifts

When people believe in the gospel of salvation, God will seal them with the Holy Spirit.

Ephesians 1:13 In whom ye also trusted, after that ye heard the word of truth, the gospel of your salvation: in whom also after that ye believed, ye were sealed with that holy Spirit of promise,

Scripture says that this seal, given by the Holy Spirit, is a key seal. Believers are being prepared to receive spiritual gifts through this key seal.

2 Corinthians 5:5 Now he that hath wrought us for the selfsame thing is God, who also hath given unto us the earnest of the Spirit.

In Greek, "earnest of the Spirit" is called arrhabōn (ἀῤῥαβών-arrhabōn). This means that it was given as an advance. The seal of the Holy Spirit is like an advance given. The first advance is like a small amount. We must add to the small amount with fruits, gifts, and power. Believers should not stop with this mere advance. It is also God's will to receive more gifts, fruits and power with this advance. So, everyone should desire gifts (1 Corinthians 14: 1). Manifestations of the Spirit are the likeness seal of God. These gifts are also the likeness seal of God. These manifestations of the Spirit are given for the benefit of eachone. Everyone can get the seal of the gifts. So, everyone should desire gifts.

1 Corinthians 12:7 But the manifestation of the Spirit is given to every man to profit withal.

Everyone wants benefits. Therefore, every believer must be prepared to receive the manifestations of the Spirit. Paul describes the gifts of the Spirit. These gifts must be received and added with the Spirit of advance.

1 Corinthians 12:8-11 For to one is given by the Spirit the word of wisdom; to another the word of knowledge by the same Spirit; To another faith by the same Spirit; to another the gifts of healing by the same Spirit; To another the working of miracles; to another prophecy; to another discerning of spirits; to another divers kinds of tongues; to another the interpretation of tongues: But all these worketh that one and the selfsame Spirit, dividing to every man severally as he will.

Take into account how wonderfully the Lord Jesus has provided miracles for believers through his death on the cross. Many people ignore this. Don't be tricked by Satan. Start examining your seals today. Because the Lord has paid a high price for you, don't ignore them. You will be given God's seals. You are encouraged to receive the Holy Spirit's gifts and to shine. This is one of my favourite Tamil Christian song lyrics.

"Decorate me with the gifts to arise and shine

Give me the complete fruits right now"

God adorns believers with gifts. So believers should pray for the Spirit of God to adorn them with gifts. May the Lord bless you! Amen.

Re-Engineering Of Holiness

God is Holy. Holiness is the likeness of God. Adam had received the same likeness when he was created. But by sinning he lost the holy likeness of God. Christ Jesus washed away sins of believers with His blood and transformed the sinful likeness of believers to the holy likeness of God.

1Peter 2:9 But ye are a chosen generation, a royal priesthood, an holy nation, a peculiar people; that ye should shew forth the praises of him who hath called you out of darkness into his marvellous light:

Christ Jesus not only washed with his blood but told believers to be holy like him.

1Peter 1:15-16 But as he which hath called you is holy, so be ye holy in all manner of conversation; Because it is written, Be ye holy; for I am holy.

The holy likeness of God, through Jesus Christ, came to man. So believers are once again embodied in the likeness of God.

Re-Engineering Of Righteousness

Man, no matter how much he claims to be righteous, he is unjust. There is no such thing as a righteous person in the world. Christ Jesus cleansed believers with His blood and conferred righteousness on them.

Philippians 3:9 And be found in him, not having mine own righteousness, which is of the law, but that which is through the faith of Christ, the righteousness which is of God by faith:

2Corinthians 5:21 For he hath made him to be sin for us, who knew no sin; that we might be made the righteousness of God in him.

1 Corinthians 1:30-31 But of him are ye in Christ Jesus, who of God is made unto us wisdom, and righteousness, and sanctification, and redemption: That, according as it is written, He that glorieth, let him glory in the Lord.

When Jesus Christ gave His righteousness to His children, those who were born again got back Adam's lost likeness of righteousness. The seal of the likeness of the righteousness of God is reappeared in men again.

❖

RE-ENGINEERING OF HUMANITY

Re-Engineering Of The Spirit

Warning: After being saved, your spirit must honor your soul as a real man, as a master, and as a person. The soul conceals the secrets as a leader. Your spirit must respect every emotion of the soul, and work powerfully to accomplish the will of the soul. The Spirit must be active, faithful, self-controlled and energetic to the soul.

Just as the Holy Spirit does not do the will of Jesus Christ, but the will of the Father, so the believers Spirit should not do the will of the fleshy body, but should do the will of their soul. thus, they get back the seal of the Triune Creator God.

Re-Engineering Of The Soul

What happened on the day Adam sinned?

The true man soul gives life, gives the word, gives deeds, loves to the physical body, and also glorifies it. As a result, the soul became the physical body's master. thus, the soul is greater than the physical body. The soul must function in the same way that God the Father does. But in contrast to this, w hen Adam sinned, the physical body became the master of the soul, and the soul became the slave of the physical body. As a result, Adam lost likeness of the Father and Jesus Christ in him.

What should happen after the salvation of believers?

After the salvation of believers, they should crucify the desires of the flesh, the lusts of the flesh, and the pride of the flesh. Believers should crucify the pride of their color of their skin, the pride of the lusts of the flesh, pride of their racism, and the pride of the beauty of the flesh. And all these should not be taken into account more than the soul. If not, all these things will make the flesh to be the lord of the soul. So the domination of the fleshy body must be controlled.

Galatians 5:24 And they that are Christ's have crucified the flesh with the affections and lusts.

If you do not crucify your fleshly desires and lusts, they will rebel against your soul and destroy the likeness of God in you. The physical body-like Jesus Christ obeyed God the soul-like Father. Similar to this, Adam's physical body was designed to elevate the soul, submit to the soul, and carry out the will of the soul. It is only intended to speak the words of the soul and carry out the will of the soul.

Just as Jesus Christ obeyed God the Father by keeping Him in the highest place, believers' physical body must keep the soul in the highest place by doing the works of the soul and speaking the words of the soul. The fleshy body should never dominate the soul.

If the body of believers obey and do the works of the soul, their bodies and souls would have the likeness of God the Father and Jesus Christ.

Re-Engineering Of The Working Body

In triune God, whatever the soul-like God said, the body-like God completed that work. Similarly, after man is saved from the sin, the body of man must do only what the soul of man says. Jesus Christ has always done nothing in violation of God the Father's directions. Likewise, the body of man should not do anything beyond the soul. The human body has to do only what the human soul does. It is the seal of the likeness of God.

After the sins have been washed away and the earnest of the Spirit is received, the likeness of the body and the soul of man started becoming like the Father and Jesus Christ. thus, the likeness of God is once again imprinted on humans.

Re-Engineering Of The Speaking Body

Whatever the soul-like God said, the body-like God said as well. Similarly, once man is saved from sin, his body must only speak what his soul says. Nothing Jesus Christ has ever said has been contrary to

God the Father's instructions. Similarly, the body of man should not say anything other than what the soul says. Only what the human soul says can be spoken by the human body. It is a representation of God's likeness.

After sins are washed away and the earnest of the Spirit is received, man's body and soul take on the likeness of the Father and Jesus Christ. The likeness of God has been imprinted on humans once again.

Re-Engineering Of Body Of Light

All who are saved are redeemed for God. This is the redemption of the soul.

Ephesians 1:13-14 In whom ye also trusted, after that ye heard the word of truth, the gospel of your salvation: in whom also after that ye believed, ye were sealed with that holy Spirit of promise, Which is the earnest of our inheritance until the redemption of the purchased possession, unto the praise of his glory.

But there is another important recovery. That is the redemption of a new body for souls. This redemption will be made as glorious to God.

We've seen that earnest of spirit is the advance sum or advance money paid for the day of redemption, so man has to be released from the perishable fleshly body to redeem the spiritual immortal body. Those who have received the earnest of the Spirit are waiting to receive this glorious body of light.

Romans 8:23 And not only they, but ourselves also, which have the firstfruits of the Spirit, even we ourselves groan within ourselves, waiting for the adoption, to wit, the redemption of our body.

Ephesians 1:14 Which is the earnest of our inheritance until the redemption of the purchased possession, unto the praise of his glory.

There is only one home for every soul on this planet, and that home is nothing more than man's fleshy body. This is the residence of the real man soul. According to the Apostle Paul, the human body that the soul wears is the earthly tent (body). This is the soul's "home" or "blanket." All humans are burdened by their earthly home (physical body). This earthly home deceives the soul, causing it to sin. This drags the soul into fleshy desires and fleshy pride. This earthly tabernacle gets illness, fatigue, disability, ageing, and burdens. It is this body that deceives soul and also curses soul.

2Corinthians 5:1-8 For we know that if our earthly house of this tabernacle were dissolved, we've a building of God, an house not made with hands, eternal in the heavens. For in this we groan, earnestly desiring to be clothed upon with our house which is from heaven: If so be that being clothed we shall not be found naked. For we that are in this tabernacle do groan, being burdened: not for that we would be unclothed, but clothed upon, that mortality might be swallowed up of life. Now he that hath wrought us for the selfsame thing is God, who also hath given unto us the earnest of the Spirit. Therefore we are always confident, knowing that, whilst we are at home in the body, we are absent from the Lord: (For we walk by faith, not by sight:) We are confident, I say, and willing rather to be absent from the body, and to be present with the Lord. Wherefore we labour, that, whether present or absent, we may be accepted of him.

According to Paul, while the outward man decays, the inner man is renewed day by day (2 Corinthians 4:16). The inner man is the human soul, and the outer man is the human body. The human soul longs to live in the new body by dismantling this painful, sick, exhausted, disabled, tired, and old physical body. But God has a time for everything, and the earnest of the Spirit has assured that the souls will receive a new immortal body in the appointed time.

God the Father has His own image (Jesus). The body-like Jesus is immortal and does not give the Father any pain, sickness, discomfort, disability, tiredness, and old age. The soul-like Father dwells in physical body-like Jesus Christ. In His likeness, God will give human soul the immortal, painless, non-sick, tireless, abled, perfect and always new body to the believers. Believers should not grieve the Holy Spirit which is given as a seal in man until the day of redemption of body of glory.

Ephesians 4:30 And grieve not the holy Spirit of God, whereby ye are sealed unto the day of redemption.

The Lord Jesus Christ, by His death, brought man and God together. The Holy Spirit descended on man. Yet, many may ask why those who are now filled with the Spirit of God do not appear as light. There are two reasons for this. First, Scripture tells us that the spirit that is now given to man is an advance.

2Corinthians 1:22 Who hath also sealed us, and given the earnest of the Spirit in our hearts.

God is about to give the body of Light in eternity; the earnest of the Spirit will serve as a hub. Therefore , man does not have a body of light on Earth. Second, why is the earnestness of the Spirit not visible to humans? It is due to the corruption of human flesh. When the human body dies and the transfiguration occurs, those who have been saved by Jesus Christ will shine like the sun in heaven. They'll be as light as Adam was.

Daniel 12:2-3 And many of them that sleep in the dust of the earth shall awake, some to everlasting life, and some to shame and everlasting contempt. And they that be wise shall shine as the brightness of the firmament; and they that turn many to righteousness as the stars forever and ever.

Adam had lost the likeness of the light. But the righteous who are called and saved by Christ (Romans 8:30) will shine like a light in the kingdom of God.

Mat 13:43 Then shall the righteous shine forth as the sun in the kingdom of their Father. Who hath ears to hear, let him hear.

God wants every believer to be changed in the likeness of Jesus Christ.

1John 3:2 Beloved, now are we the sons of God, and it doth not yet appear what we shall be: but we know that, when he shall appear, we shall be like him; for we shall see him as he is.

Thus the full divine likeness and image of God will be restored to man.

❖

THE DEATH OF ILLUSION

"All are lunatics, but he who can analyze his delusion is called a philosopher."— Ambrose Bierce,

You would have heard as follows...

Our existence is a delusion...

Everything appears to be an illusion or delusion.

This world is a lie....

Everything in this world is deception...

In this world, no one is permanent...

This world is a stage for drama...

Most spiritualists, scientists, and philosophers in this world have no answer for illusion. This is the only place where the entire world is trapped. You've probably heard spiritualists from various religions claim that everything is an illusion. Solomon, the world's greatest wise man, once said that everything is illusory and disturbing. What exactly is illusion? Illusion is filled everywhere. Existing things will disappear without it, this is illusion. Illusion is terrible. Illusion is painful. Everyone is trapped within this illusion. Illusion swallows everything. It is the illusion that human beings die in this world. It is illusion that swallows even the insect and also the great galaxies sparing not them. The illusion is a mystery that the world should fear. Illusion devours everything in this world. It is an illusion that people die in this world. It is illusion that swallows even a small insect and the great galaxies without mercy. The illusion is a mystery that the world should be afraid of. Everything in this world is devoured by illusion. When did the illusion begin? When will the illusion come to an end? Will this illusion last? Why does the illusion not spare even those who seek love, the light, the truth, peace, happiness, and God?

We will go into greater detail about how the Holy Bible shed light on the mysteries of illusion theory. We will also see the close relationship between God's seals in man and the existence of illusion.

<u>The origin and purpose of illusion:</u> The first man ate the fruit of the tree of knowing good and evil, thinking he would become a god through the serpent's advice. The first man appeared as a small god in light clothing. This is because he was created in the image and likeness of God. But the moment he ate the fruit, he became a slave to the world he ruled. He lost the seal that God had given him, as well as all the goodness of the Holy Spirit. This shining first man had lost his shining glorious body. God took a look at the man who had lost his glorious image and likeness. God gave Adam and his descendants the

rapidly fading illusion that they couldn't live in this world for long. God subjected the entire nature and everything in it to the rapidly fading illusion. This is how the illusion began. Humans began to perish. The purpose of illusion is to swallow everything.

Genesis 3:19 In the sweat of thy face shalt thou eat bread, till thou return unto the ground; for out of it wast thou taken: for dust thou art, and unto dust shalt thou return.

The illusion fastened humans and the world. Birds, land animals, aquatic animals and plants have died under the rule of this illusion. Nothing in the world could escape from the clutches of illusion.

Genesis 3:17 And unto Adam he said, Because thou hast hearkened unto the voice of thy wife, and hast eaten of the tree, of which I commanded thee, saying, Thou shalt not eat of it: cursed is the ground for thy sake; in sorrow shalt thou eat of it all the days of thy life;

The universe is expanding and new things are being created on one side. The black hole, on the other hand, is devouring the universe. As a result, illusion devours the entire universe. Why is the world destined to be like this? What causes everything to vanish? People claim that everything is an illusion because there is the mystery that nothing permanent exists in this world.

People are now so enslaved to illusion that they cannot even comprehend this.

Groaning, Watching And Freedom From Illusion

Before sinning, Adam was a God-fearing man with all the seals of God. He was glorious with the likeness of God. But Adam lost his status as son of God when he lost the key seal. All the creatures on the earth which had been given to Adam became slave to illusion.

When people are redeemed by the blood of Jesus, they come with all the seals of God, then, all creatures will be redeemed from their bondage to illusion. Jesus is the one who created the illusion, and Jesus is the one who destroys the illusion. On the day of redemption, mankind will be freed from the corrupted fleshy body and redeem the body of the immortal light. It is the redemption of the body of light. For the day of this redemption, the Holy Spirit of God is given as a seal.

Ephesians 4:30 And grieve not the holy Spirit of God, whereby ye are sealed unto the day of redemption.

The world is waiting for such redemption; and the believers who have received the first fruits of the Spirit are also waiting for the redemption of the immortal body by the same Spirit.

Romans 8:23-24 And not only they, but ourselves also, which have the firstfruits of the Spirit, even we ourselves groan within ourselves, waiting for the adoption, to wit, the redemption of our body. For we are saved by hope: but hope that is seen is not hope: for what a man seeth, why doth he yet hope for?

When Christ is revealed, the sons of God who were dead in Christ will appear in immortal bodies that are the body of light. Every creature is waiting for the sons of God to appear.

Romans 8:19 For the earnest expectation of the creature waiteth for the manifestation of the sons of God.

Every creature (Tree, Plant, Cody, Animals, Insects, Birds, Living Water, Stone, Soil, Rock, Air, Water, Sun, Moon, Planets, Stars, and Galaxies) is waiting for the revelation of the sons of God. Those who will be wearing the body of light are the sons of God. Until then, they are all subject to the illusion and suffer with a birth pang. When they see the sons of God appearing in God's complete image and likeness of Go with new immortal bodies of light, then the world will be freed from the bondage of illusion. After that, a new earth and heaven will also appear.New land animals, new birds, new aquatic animals, and new plants also will appear. The world and the things in it become immortal without the illusion. Then the word illusion will be utterly destroyed. There will be no illusion again. Therefore, all creatures are waiting with agony as to when and how the sons of God will manifest and when the illusion will disappear. Until then, all creatures are subject to deadly illusion.

Rom 8:21 Because the creature itself also shall be delivered from the bondage of corruption into the glorious liberty of the children of God.

Rom 8:22 For we know that the whole creation groaneth and travaileth in pain together until now.

These days, everyone in the world would say that everything is an illusion. Be careful! In this world, you are the slave of illusion! Even if a man goes to hell, he is not free from illusion. If you want to be free from illusion, you must be born again out of the womb of Dead-Karma (sin) into the world of Spirit and light, be washed with the blood of Jesus, receive the seal of Spirit of God, and keep the Spirit until you receive the body of glorious light. When you receive a new immortal body, the illusion frees you. Otherwise, you will be a slave to illusion. It will destroy you just little by little. No one will be able to escape the harsh rule of illusion in this world! BEWARE!

DANGERS OF IGNORING THE WARNING

Beware! Your Silver Cord Will Be Loosed

Death is the most terrible of all things, for it is the end, and nothing is thought to be either good or bad for the dead

- Aristotle

It is the will of God that every man must have the divine seal of the God. The most important worship is to have the complete seals of God in man, and other than this, there is no other important worship. The book Ecclesiastes describes how the life of every man who rejects the will of God will be. At the beginning of this book we read that everything is vanity (illusion). The main objective of this book is that all life without God's seal is an illusion. In this book, there is a scripture with a deeper meaning,

Ecc 12:6-8 Or ever the silver cord be loosed, or the golden bowl be broken, or the pitcher be broken at the fountain, or the wheel broken at the cistern. Then shall the dust return to the earth as it was: and the spirit shall return unto God who gave it. Vanity of vanities, saith the preacher; all is vanity.

Pay close attention to this passage. The wise man Solomon wrote about how the body eventually returns to the soil. There are four ways the body might re-enter the earth. Everyone is cautioned in this passage to consider God before returning to the soil.

- The silver cord be loosed
- The golden bowl be broken
- The pitcher be broken at the fountain
- The wheel broken at the cistern

Let us see what all these mean.

The silver cord is the spirit of man. The silver cord binds the physical body and soul of man together. As long as the physical body is attached to the soul, the soul completes its work through the physical body. The physical body lives by the soul. When the silver cord of man is loosened, the physical body and the soul are separated. Then the physical body dies and returns to the soil.

The silver cord of the Lord Jesus Christ at the time of death was loosened. That is, His spirit left him. So He cried unto the Father as follows:

Matthew 27:50 Jesus, when he had cried again with a loud voice, yielded up the spirit.

Giving up one's spirit is nothing but the loosening of the cord that binds the soul and the physical body.Immediately after loosening the silver cord the life departs man. The life, the spirit, and the silver cord are the same thing.

Moreover, Scripture also calls this spirit as light.

Proverbs 20:27 The spirit of a man is the lamp of the LORD,

There is a spirit within every man that is like light. For this reason, many people in the Eastern nations will light their homes with lamps when a man dies. Man can be transformed by the power of God as long as this silver cord is with him because the spirit serves as an ambassador to the divine world. As long as the silver cord serves as a channel of communication between people and God, people must be cleansed by the blood of Jesus Christ and saved. It is challenging to join the Kingdom of God and be saved once the silver cord has left a man. Once the silver cord leaves him, the communication to the divine world will be disconnected. So no one can be saved by Jesus Christ, and it is not possible to receive God's seals. Everyone must be made aware about the end of their life.

If the silver cord of man leaves from him, man will not be able to obtain salvation and also can not get the sealing of the Spirit. Do you want to be washed with the blood of Jesus and shine with seals or are you going to die cruelly?

Golden Bowl Will Be Broken

In the Temple built by Solomon, lamps were made of gold. These golden lamps were lightened using oil. This golden lamp used to burn and give light because there was oil in it.

Exodus 25:31 And thou shalt make a candlestick of pure gold: of beaten work shall the candlestick be made: his shaft, and his branches, his bowls, his knops, and his flowers, shall be of the same.

In the Temple of God, there were seven lamps in single lamp stand. These seven lamps are seven Spirits of God. Man's physical body is golden bowl. Likewise, man must have seven Spirits of God upon him.

The spirit is the light and this light is spirit. The spirit of man burns as a light. Golden bowl is the body of man. The soul never breaks. It is eternal. Only God can destroy it. The body can be destroyed at anytime by anyone. When the body is broken the spirit leaves the body. The soul also separates from the body. The word "Silver cord be loosed" is written in Hebrew as raw-khak. This means eliminating or withdrawing. The golden bowl of man (body) is also breakable. You can break it anytime. The light will go away from you when the golden bowl is broken. Your soul must receive the seals of the Spirit of God before your light leaves you.

Pitcher Will Be Broken

Man dies the moment his spirit departs from him. Following the breakdown of the body's tissues, body fluids and gases will be released, filling the corpse. The human body has several glands that release bodily fluids, including blood glands, acid glands, and harmonic glands. The pitchers that trigger these tiny glands are broken when a man physically dies. From this moment on, the human body begins to decompose. The fleshy body will be blown inside the corpses like a balloon when the body's gases and bodily fluids are released. When the body fluids and gases are pressurized within, they will pass through the cavities of the human body. Now, the foul smell of the corpse will be unbearable. This is what happens when the pitcher is broken, human body begins to perish. Your soul must receive the seals of the Spirit of

God before the physical body is decomposed. Beware! You cannot reverse anything to save the soul after the pitcher is broken.

Wheel Will Be Broken

When a man's body is dead, the interior of the body starts to decompose and it starts to smell bad. Inside the corpse, gases like hydrogen sulphide, carbon dioxide, methane, and nitrogen will form and fill it with high pressure. Beginning with the abdomen, the body swells more. The gates (wheels) of the mouth, nose, faeces holes, and urinary holes break down when the corpse is highly pressurised by body fluids and gases. The gates (wheels) are damaged in this way, and the body disintegrates. The physical body of a man can be ruthlessly destroyed in this way. Before the gates (wheels) of your body start to break down, your soul must receive the Spirit of God's seals.

Soul May Be Left Alone In Horror

You must keep in mind your creator before your silver cord becomes loosened, before your golden bowl breaks, before your pitcher breaks, and before your wheel breaks. Beware! After all these are broken, nothing can be reversed. When these are shattered, man's spirit will turn to God. Man's dead body will eventually rot in the ground.

Job 34:14-15 If he set his heart upon man, if he gather unto himself his spirit and his breath; All flesh shall perish together, and man shall turn again unto dust.

If the physical body of man leaves the soul, the soul of man will be left alone. The status of such a man will be miserable. Below, you will find out what the state of the human soul is like.

Ecclesiastes 9:10 Whatever your hand finds to do, do it with all your might, for in the realm of the dead, where you are going, there is neither working nor planning nor knowledge nor wisdom.

1. It is man's body that works for his soul. Because the body departs from the soul at death, the soul cannot perform any physical work on its own. When a man dies in the flesh, his works cease (Ecclesiastes 9:10). As a result, the soul is dormant and incapable of functioning.

2. When the soul is separated from its physical body, it is unable to plan anything (Ecclesiastes 9:10). The word "planning" means "intelligence" in Hebrew. Only when man's mind and spirit unite can soul think. As a result, after the body and spirit of man have left the soul, the soul cannot make any plans.

3. Because the body departs from the soul at death, the soul lacks worldly knowledge. In this world, man can learn as much as he wants. However, the soul, which is separate from the body and spirit, will not have any of those learned knowledges. All of these insights are the result of the body and spirit working together. Thus, worldly knowledge vanishes with the body and spirit; after death, the soul will lose worldly knowledge (Ecclesiastes 9:10).

4. There would be no worldly wisdom after the soul is separated from the spirit and the body. As a result, the soul loses its worldly wisdom after death (Ecclesiastes 9:10).

5. The soul that has lost its body and spirit will not require any earthly food. Because there is no physical body, the soul cannot taste. As a result, the soul does not require earthly nourishment (Rev. 18:14).

6. Those who are alive are aware that they will perish. However, the souls of those who have died in the body are unable to know anything because they are unable to gain knowledge or wisdom. They will have no visions, dreams, or knowledge if they do not have the spirit. They will not be given any revelations (Ecclesiastes 9: 5). This is why Jesus went to Hades to preach to the souls, because the souls could not understand that Jesus died for them.

1 Peter 3:19 And he preached to those souls who were held in Sheol (Aramaic Bible in Plain English)

7. Do you know what the works of the flesh are? Worldly friendship, Adultery, fornication, uncleanness, lasciviousness, idolatry, witchcraft, hatred, variance, emulations, wrath, strife, seditions, heresies, envying, murders, drunkenness, retellings, and such are all the works of the flesh (Galatians 5: 19-21). How can souls without a fleshy body perform these works if there is no fleshy body? The abandoned soul cannot have fleshly works.

8. The soul that has been separated from the flesh has no place on earth (Ecclesiastes 9: 6). All of their lust, hatred, and jealousy have vanished; they have no part in anything under the sun anymore.

Look at this horror! The soul is left alone after death, without the body or the spirit. Many people on this planet commit suicide because they are lonely. In reality, they are not alone. They have spirit and body as companions. People could have developed a very strong connection with God through their Spirit and been saved, but now the soul suffers from loneliness in the absence of body and spirit. It's dreadful! The state of those who die without receiving the full Divine Seal is dreadful. Physical death may be terrifying for many people. But the death of the soul will be horrifying. So, what should everyone do as long as they live on this planet?

Seek God while your physical body and spirit are with you.

Do good works while your spirit and your physical body are attached to the soul. Otherwise, you can't do anything until you get your new body.

Worship God in spirit while your spirit is with you

Pray in the spirit while your spirit is with you

Physically work very well while your physical body is with you

Test whether you have the Spirit of God in you

Test whether you have received the seals of the Spirit and that they are active

You May Not Have Known This Difference

When a man dies, there will be a very important difference between a saved soul and an unsaved soul. That difference is the earnest seal of the Holy Spirit. The Holy Spirit abides in the saved soul even after a man dies.

John 14:16 And I will pray the Father, and he shall give you another Comforter, that he may abide with you for ever;

The seal will remain intact in the redeemed man. Which day is the day of redemption? The day of redemption is the day of redemption of his glorious body of light. Until then, the soul will be unclothed. Only those with the earnest seals of the Holy Spirit, also known as the hub of receiving the glorious body of light, will be able to enter heaven and receive that body.

Ephesians 1:13-14 In whom ye also trusted, after that ye heard the word of truth, the gospel of your salvation: in whom also after that ye believed, ye were sealed with that holy Spirit of promise, Which is the earnest of our inheritance until the redemption of the purchased possession, unto the praise of his glory. .

2Corinthians 1:22 Who hath also sealed us, and given the earnest of the Spirit in our hearts.

Ephesians 4:30 And grieve not the holy Spirit of God, whereby ye are sealed unto the day of redemption.

The seals of the Spirit, according to scripture, remain in the soul of the saved man, even after his physical death. So the Spirit's earnest seal remains in man for the redemption of his glorious body of light. This seal is not available to those who have not been saved and have not received the earnest seal of the Holy Spirit.

Beware!Life Review Is Waiting

Examine what happens after your sins are washed away by blood of Jesus. After the soul is separated from the body, worldly knowledge and wisdom are lost, but man is carried into a "life review" process by the waves of the new life. During this time, you will be able to see your entire life history, from birth to death. There, you will see your own film. You will be programmed to look back over your life. All of your previous thoughts, feelings, emotions, actions, spoken words, and missed opportunities will be brought back to life and placed in front of your conscience. Everyone is born with a sinful nature. Nobody is blameless. Every man's sin follows him from birth to death like a dark cloud. Nothing will be held back. Conscience depicts a man's life without forgetting anything he has forgotten in physical life. You would have punished someone, hurt many, deceived many, failed to help the needy, were lazy, unbelieving, hopeless, dishonest, and so on. When you consider all of this, you will be ashamed and filthy for having such a guilty conscience. Wouldn't heaven be hell if the guilty conscience was there? The world was mentally frozen during Adam's first death, when man stood naked, losing his body of light. Man loses his physical body and his soul stands naked during the second death of people. The third death will not be like this. The soul will die alone in its cruel death. His conscience will kill him, and he will never return. Alas! It will be an abandoned day! The Lord Jesus Christ came to this world and shed His blood to save the soul from the wrath of God.

The blood of Jesus Christ which has the eternal Spirit is capable of cleaning your conscience from dead works. The blood of Jesus Christ is something that can sanctify your soul, also cleanse your guilty conscience, and redeem it.

Hebrews 9:14 How much more shall the blood of Christ, who through the eternal Spirit offered himself without spot to God, purge your conscience from dead works to serve the living God?

If you are washed with the blood of Jesus Christ, the dead works (sin) will be completely removed from your conscience.You cannot trace out your Dead-Works (sin) in your conscience.

What a gift! What a blessing! Look how lovely it is! In this universe, there is only one God. Do not regard Jesus Christ as an alien God. You have Jesus Christ's likeness seal. He is your personal deity. The likeness seal of Jesus Christ within you is revolutionary proof that you belong to Him! Don't be deceived! Your religion will not accompany you. If you are not washed by the blood of Jesus, You will be accompanied by your Dead-Karma (sin). Who is going to save you? What will happen to you after you die? What lies ahead for you? Think about these:

1John 1:7 … the blood of Jesus Christ his Son cleanseth us from all sin.

1 John 1:8 If we say that we've no sin, we deceive ourselves, and the truth is not in us.

1 John 1:9 If we confess our sins, he is faithful and just to forgive us our sins, and to cleanse us from all unrighteousness.

❖

TRANSFUSION A SIN?

(An Advice to Jehovah's Witnesses)

Jehovah's Witnesses strictly prohibit blood transfusions, even when such a procedure could save a person's life. They believe that receiving another person's blood introduces that person's conscience into the recipient, possibly transferring guilt and resulting in eternal punishment. Because of this, even those facing death often refuse transfusions.

However, those who are washed in the blood of Jesus Christ need not fear such things. Scripture and reason both show that receiving a blood transfusion is not sinful. Let us look closer at this matter.

The Belief About Blood And Conscience

Jehovah's Witnesses teach that blood carries a person's conscience and spiritual identity. They believe that if a donor's blood carries guilt or sin, that guilt passes to whoever receives it.

Science does confirm that blood has a "voice." In forensic studies, blood can reveal the identity of a person and serve as a silent witness in solving crimes. Symbolically, the "voice of blood" represents the voice of conscience.

But where does sin truly begin? The Bible says sin originates not in the blood, but in the heart.

Matthew 5:28 – "Whosoever looks on a woman to lust after her has already committed adultery with her in his heart."

The heart decides to sin first. The spirit in the blood may carry that decision through the body, but it does not create or transfer guilt. The voice of the blood reflects the conscience of its current possessor, not the donor.

The Voice In The Blood And The Soul

The Bible mentions the voice of blood in two important ways:

Voice in the Blood:

Genesis 4:10 – "The voice of your brother's blood cries out to me from the ground."

Voice in the Soul:

Revelation 6:10 – "They cried with a loud voice, saying, 'How long, O Lord, holy and true, until You judge and avenge our blood?'"

In both verses, blood and soul speak alike. This shows that the conscience resides in the soul, not in the physical blood. The spirit in the blood reflects the soul's voice, but it does not carry an independent or transferable conscience.

When blood is donated, it carries traces of the donor's physical life, not his soul. Once transfused into another person, the blood immediately harmonizes with the recipient's spirit and conscience. It takes on the identity of the one in whom it now flows.

Therefore, transfused blood does not transfer another person's sin or guilt. The court of conscience is established by God in each person's soul, and it cannot be replaced by anyone else's conscience.

Life In The Blood

Leviticus 17:11 – "For the life of the flesh is in the blood."

This verse teaches that the life (the spirit) is in the blood. The human spirit is an extraordinary part of God's creation. It connects the physical and the spiritual. When transfused blood enters another body, it takes on that person's spirit and life-force. The blood adjusts to the new body and receives the new conscience.

Thus, there is no spiritual harm in accepting blood from another person. Instead, it becomes part of the recipient's living system and obeys the voice of their own soul.

The Cleansing Blood Of Christ

If anyone still fears that another's blood might carry guilt, Scripture provides assurance:

1 John 1:7 – "The blood of Jesus Christ His Son cleanses us from all sin."

The blood of Jesus is all-powerful. It purifies believers from every sin and dead work. It also speaks better things than the blood of Abel, which cried out for vengeance.

Hebrews 12:24 – "And to Jesus the mediator of the new covenant, and to the blood of sprinkling, that speaks better things than that of Abel."

The blood of Christ knows exactly whose sins it covers. It does not confuse the conscience of one person with another. Each conscience remains individual and accountable only to God.

Therefore, for believers — including Jehovah's Witnesses — there is nothing sinful about receiving a blood transfusion. The conscience of another cannot condemn you, for the blood of Christ has already cleansed your soul and made you pure before God.

Conclusion

Blood transfusion is a medical gift, not a spiritual curse. The blood itself does not carry another person's guilt. When it enters a new body, it aligns with the recipient's spirit and conscience.

More importantly, those who are in Christ are protected by His redeeming blood, which cleanses every sin and silences all accusations of guilt.

Thus, refusing a transfusion out of fear of sin is unnecessary. Faith in the blood of Jesus Christ is far greater than any fear of human blood. His blood speaks mercy, forgiveness, and life — not condemnation.

***

REFERENCES

Thirukkural

Hadith Qudsi

Wikipedia

Aghora III: The Law of Karma p ,43Robert E Svoboda, Published by Brotherwood of Life Inc., & Sadhana Publication Texas, USA

Create Your Own Net Worth by Sunday Adelaja,

Rise Up and Salute the Sun: The Writings of Suzy Kassem

Pirkei Avot

Dhammapada – Sayings of the Buddha 1 (translation by J. Richards)

Phaenom, v. 5, poem of Aratus

Quaran

Encyclopedia-of-islam Page-342

The Book of Zakat, (Richness does not lie in the abundance of (worldly) goods but richness is the richness of the soul)

Raquel: Beyond the Cleavage 768Wikiquote

Upanishads vol. 2, Brihadaranyaka-Upanishad Part 3

E-Sword, Electronic edge

Nature, international journal of science, article published on 17 january 2018

Vivekananda, in Complete Works, Volume 2, p.88

Charles William Stubbs, Alone with my conscience

The Bhagavata Purana , Srimad Bhagavatam

Candlesticks, fibonacci, and chart pattern trading tools, r o b e r t f i s c h e r, j e n s f i s c h e r

William Shakespeare, Richard III (c. (1591, Act V, scene 3, line .193

Hindu, Laws of Manu chapter 7

The Vishnu Purana - Chapter VI

THE FUNERARY SACRIFICE OF ANMALS DURLNG THE PREDYNASTIC PERIOD, Rsearch done in Egypt and the Thesis submitted by Diane Victoria Flores

The ante-Nicene fathers, The Christian Literature Publishing Co. p. 136.

Leon Battista Alberti, : TheThree Books of Painting, 1435

Tertullian. "Apologeticum"

A History of New Testament Times by Paul Barnett 2002 ISBN 0-8308-2699-8 page 30

Jesus outside the New Testament: an introduction to the ancient evidence by Robert E. Van Voorst 2000

Jesus Remembered by James D. G. Dunn 2003 ISBN 0-8028-3931-2 page 339

An early first-century earthquake in the Dead Sea, https://www.researchgate.net/publication/229810999

Thomas Brooks in A Cabinet of Jewels (1669) from Works of Thomas Brooks, Vol. 3, Nichol's Series of Standard Divines, Puritan Period, with General Preface by John C. Miller, D.D.; Rev. Thomas Smith, General Editor, Edinburgh, James Nichol, 1866. pg.295

www.ingramcontent.com/pod-product-compliance
Ingram Content Group UK Ltd.
Pitfield, Milton Keynes, MK11 3LW, UK
UKHW021344190726
13845UKWH00027B/715

9 788199 511590